TIGER WOODS

2001: THE YEAR OF THE TIGER

GRAND SLAM EDITION

Tiger Woods
2001: The Year Of The Tiger

This publication is not sponsored or endorsed by, or otherwise affiliated with Tiger Woods or any of his affiliates, subsidiaries, distributors or representatives. Some of the items depicted within this publication are trademarked and are the sole property of their owner. Any opinions expressed are solely those of the authors, and do not necessarily reflect those of Tiger Woods.

Photo Credits: front cover – clockwise from top: Reuters NewMedia Inc./CORBIS, AP/WWP, AFP/CORBIS; back cover – AP/WWP; page 1 – AP/WWP

EDITORIAL

Managing Editor: Jeff Mahony
Associate Editors: Melissa A. Bennett
Gia C. Manalio
Mike Micciulla
Paula Stuckart
Assistant Editors: Heather N. Carreiro
Jennifer Renk
Joan C. Wheal
Editorial Assistants: Timothy R. Affleck
Beth Hackett
Christina M. Sette
Steven Shinkaruk

PRODUCTION

Production Manager: Scott Sierakowski

ART

Creative Director: Joe T. Nguyen
Assistant Art Director: Lance Doyle
Senior Graphic Designers: Marla B. Gladstone
Susannah C. Judd
David S. Maloney
Carole Mattia-Slater
David Ten Eyck
Graphic Designers: Jennifer J. Bennett
Sean-Ryan Dudley
Kimberly Eastman
Melani Gonzalez
Jim MacLeod
Jeremy Maendel
Chery-Ann Poudrier

R&D

Product Development
Manager: Paul Rasid

ISBN 1-58598-224-5

CheckerBee
PUBLISHING
306 Industrial Park Road
Middletown, CT 06457

CollectorsQuest
•com

Table Of Contents

5   Welcome To The World Of Tiger Woods

6   *A True Master*

7   The Tiger Phenomenon

16   *2001: The Year Of The Tiger*

17   Four-In-A-Row! The 2001 Masters

23   Tiger And The Grand Slam

27   Prelude To Victory

30   *The Makings Of A Grand Slam*

31   The Masters

35   The U.S. Open

39   The British Open

43   The PGA Championship

46   *The Man*

47   Tiger's Story

63   Hanging Out With Tiger

69   Tiger Tales

74   *The Legend*

75   The Bond Of A Lifetime

80   The Zen Of Tiger

86   The Secrets Of Tiger's Success

91   Tiger's Tools

95   Tiger Trivia

Table Of Contents

98   *A Record Of Excellence*

99   Career Statistics

100   PGA Victories

102   Great Moments In Tiger's Career

110   Tiger's Trophies

114   *Golf Through The Years*

115   History Of Golf

123   Legends Of Golf

130   *Tiger And The Game*

131   The PGA

140   PGA Courses

149   Tiger's Challengers

154   Great LPGA Players Of Today

156   *A Fan-tastic Sport*

157   The Tournament Day Experience

165   Keeping Up With Tiger

172   The Endorsement King

178   Tiger's Products

183   Tiger Memorabilia

187   A Golf Glossary

190   Photo Index

Welcome To The World Of Tiger Woods

When Tiger Woods steps to the tee, fans shudder in awe and anticipation as each swing from his mighty club makes an old record come crashing down. This special Grand Slam Edition of the CheckerBee Fan Guide™ to Tiger Woods is a celebration of one the greatest athletes ever to play the game.

Inside this special edition of the CheckerBee Fan Guide™ series, you'll enjoy a fascinating, personal look at the life and career of Tiger Woods – the golfing phenom who has enjoyed an amazing ride to legendary status, culminating in his unique "Tiger Slam" in 2001. Whether spending a night on the town or an afternoon on the course, few athletes draw attention as easily as Tiger Woods! It's his unbeatable combination of strength, concentration and determination that has made him such a success.

If you've just caught "Tigermania" and are too new to the sport of golf for nicknames like the "Golden Bear" to ring a bell, sections spotlighting the history of golf, as well as its greatest legends, will fill you in on what you've been missing. There's also plenty of great information for veteran fans and players of the sport, including a tour of the sights and sounds you're likely to encounter on tournament day. The CheckerBee Fan Guide™ also features a fun andinformative section showcasing many of Tiger's products and memorabilia.

Tiger has done more to attract new fans to the sport than any other golfer before him. Chinese folklore may state that 2001 is the year of the snake, but readers of the *CheckerBee Fan Guide™ to Tiger Woods* will discover that 2001 is really *the year of the Tiger*!

A True Master

The Tiger Phenomenon

From the very beginning, Tiger Woods' story has been the stuff of legends. In his first 25 years, he has already become one of the most important sports figures in history. Tiger has literally changed the face of golf, and once all is said and done, he may well become the singular icon of the sport.

Many say that Tiger Woods' prowess as a player is derived from his parents' sense that their son has a date with destiny. That he has, from his youngest days, shown signs of greatness. Could it be that he is fulfilling a plan larger than his own?

His parents certainly think so. As an infant and toddler, Tiger sat in a highchair and watched his father, Earl, hit golf balls. Earl swears that as a result of this, Tiger already possessed a two-hour attention span by six months of age. Furthermore, Tiger's first golf swing was a perfect imitation of his father's. That was, by the way, at the ripe age of 11 months.

By age 5, Tiger owned a set of golf clubs. Three years later, he won his first tournament. That win came as no surprise to Tiger's parents. His mother said she instilled in him early on a take-no-prisoners approach to competition. "I said, 'Go after them, kill them,'" Tida recalled. "'When you're finished, now it's sportsmanship. Before that, go for that throat. Don't let your opponent up.'" Perhaps because of this early training, Tiger is known for his phenomenal focus in competition, his ability to

John Todd/ Newsport

Tiger rests between holes at Pebble Beach Golf Links in February 2000.

block everything else out and his skill at turning difficult situations around to his advantage. This has earned him the admiration of other golfers and golfing fans, and the respect of sports fans in general.

In addition to his drive to win, Tiger possesses a deep hatred of losing. "What is the saying, that winning never gets old," he once said. "Or put it another way: I've never enjoyed losing. That's why I work as hard as I do."

The Legend

It's hard not to love a champion, particularly when everyone who watches him feels they are observing something truly historical, a genuine phenomenon. As an amateur player, Tiger won 36 tournaments, including three U.S. Amateur Championships (1994, 1995, 1996). He was the youngest player ever to win, and the first to do so three consecutive years. In the summer of 1996, he turned pro and won two of his first eight tournaments. One of these was the 1997 Masters, where he not only won, but also annihilated the competition by a record-setting 12 strokes.

The fact that Tiger had been putting at such a young age seems to have given him a tremendous advantage. In practice, he is capable of making 100 six-foot putts consecutively with only his right hand. And off the tee, he can send a ball soaring more than 300 yards. "I can't imagine being a pro golfer

Tiger at the 1995 U.S. Amateur Golf Championship, where he wins the event for the second straight year.

and driving [the golf ball] three hundred yards and still be behind Tiger," said football quarterback Kurt Warner. "How intimidating is that?"

The sense that Tiger can accomplish the impossible has also reinforced his image as a golden child of the sport. He has consistently shown that he is capable of making shots other players would fear to attempt. "You hate to keep blowing his horn," commentator Curtis Strange once said on television, "but every time you turn around, he's doing something no one else can."

He has earned not just the awe, but also the respect, of other players. Tiger is known for being harder on himself than anyone else ever would be. He is hypercritical of his own game and sets extremely high standards for himself. He also trains hard. He runs two miles every day, even during competitions, and he performs a rigorous workout to maintain the muscle bulk he needs for his famous long drives.

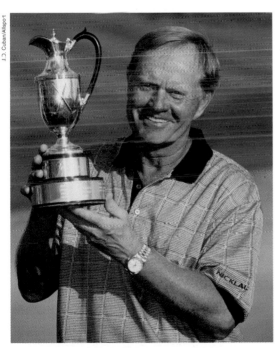

With a stellar PGA career behind him, Jack Nicklaus still enjoys victory on the Senior tour.

Early in his life, Tiger set a career goal of beating Jack Nicklaus' all-time record of 18 majors (The Masters, the U.S. Open, the British Open and the PGA Championship). Today, even Nicklaus expects to see this happen. When Tiger won his second Masters in 2001, he became the first golfer to hold all four major tournament titles at the same time.

America's Child

Golf has been known as a sport for upper-class caucasians for ages. But Tiger has broken those barriers. From his parents, he inherited Thai,

Good Advice

According to Tiger, the best advice he ever received was from his parents. They told him, "Care and share."

African-American, Native American and Chinese heritage. Somehow, it seemed appropriate to Americans watching him play that this unique representative of America's melting pot should come along and shake up a sport with a long history of discrimination.

Many golf clubs have a long history of not allowing members who are not white. In 1994, Tiger was tied for the lead with just over one hole left to play in the Jerry Pate National Intercollegiate, one of college golf's most prestigious tournaments. Standing just off the green was the Shoal Creek Golf Club's 71-year-old founder Hall Thompson, who just four years before had told a reporter that the club doesn't "discriminate in any other area except the blacks." Despite the distraction, Tiger won the tournament with a two-shot victory. After the last round, Thompson approached Tiger and said, "You are a great player. I'm proud of you. You're superb." With his skill and grace, Tiger was changing the sport of golf.

Beyond the race barrier, golf's image has been one of inaccessibility. The unstated premise of the game is that it's a sport for the rich. Tiger shattered that barrier, as well. When he first started competing in tournaments, he and his parents would fly in the morning of an event and check into a Motel 6. This allowed for little sleep and no time for a practice round.

"One day, Tiger said, 'Pop, do you think we could get to the site early enough so I could get in a practice round?'" his father said in an interview. "I thought about it,

A focused Tiger tees off at a tournament.

Tiger uses his legendary mental focus to line up an important putt.

and I said: 'Son, I apologize. I promise you from this day forward, you will have just as good of a chance as any of these country club kids, and if I have to go broke, that's what we're going to do.' From that point on, we went a day in advance, he stayed with his peers at the Marriotts and the Hiltons, and he kicked butt and took names." His mother says they "didn't want Tiger to grow up with an inferiority complex, so even if we have to take out second mortgage or home equity loan, we let him have it."

Today, Tiger has become a role model for children across the country, particularly those from minority or disadvantaged backgrounds. For the first time in the history of the game, it is truly possible for people from all walks of life to imagine seeing themselves on the golf course.

A New Game

Tiger has single-handedly changed the popularity and image of golf – and with that, the financial stakes involved. "We all ought to be thankful he's out here," said golfer Steve Pate. "Because of him we're playing for a helluva lot more money." When Tiger plays, television ratings skyrocket. Even tournaments that he doesn't play in have a huge increase in gate receipts and sponsorship revenues. "Before Tiger came along, you used to catch golf on TV every now and then," said basketball star Shaquille O'Neal. "Now they're interrupting football and basketball games to show golf. He's done a lot for the sport."

The mass popularization of the sport has also changed the crowds it brings in. Once viewed as the domain of those who spoke in whispers, golf has a new generation of fans being lured by Tiger's skill and charisma. But they have not necessarily shown themselves to be masters of golf etiquette. At the 2000 Nissan Open at the very highbrow Riviera Country Club in Pacific Palisades, California, the crowds were described by one press report as a "liquored-up circus."

"It's changing, and I like the way it's going, the way kids are getting involved," Tiger said. "But it's up to the adults to educate these kids and not get belligerently drunk on the course and mouth off. It's a double-edged sword: you want everybody to participate, but not everyone who comes out is a golfer. You get some fans who are football fans, hockey fans, basketball fans who like to do other things on the golf course."

Tiger And Sports

Tiger's favorite sports to watch and play (besides golf, of course) are baseball and basketball.

LEADERS																		
HOLE	1	2	3	4	5	6	7	8	9	10	11	12	13	14	15	16	17	18
PAR	4	5	4	3	4	3	4	5	4	4	4	3	5	4	5	3	4	4
WOODS	15	16	16	16	15	15	14	15	15	15	16	16	17	18				
ROCCA	6	7	7	7	7	6	6	6	6	6	5	5	5	5				
STANKOWSKI	5	4	3	2	2	2	3	3	2	3	2	2	2	3	3			
KITE T.	4	5	5	4	4	3	4	5	5	5	5	5	6	6	6	5		
WATSON. T.	5	6	6	6	7	6	3	4	4	5	5	6	6	6	6	5		
SLUMAN	3	3	3	3	2	2	3	3	3	3	3	3	4	5	3	3		
LOVE	0	1	0	0	1	0	0	0	0	0	0	1	3	3	4	3	3	
LANGER	2	1	2	2	2	2	1	0	1	0	0	0	1	1	2	2	2	2
COUPLES	2	3	3	3	2	1	2	2	2	2	2	2	3	1	1	2	3	
TOLLES	0	1	2	2	2	2	2	1	2	2	2	2	3	3	4	5	5	5

A crowd looks on as Tiger hits a shot out of the gallery.

His father has been more blunt: "I've got news for you: it's going to get worse, not better. Tiger is the lead tip of the new breed of golfer coming to the PGA tour. And some of these kids are coming from the ghettos; they're not privy to the Woods Finishing School. Mark my words – I've seen them. You're going to get a Rodman, a McEnroe: [He will] bitch like hell at everything, have little or no respect for the traditions of the game. He'll have qualified at qualifying school and gotten his card, so you won't be able to sit that guy on the bench. What's golf going to do then?"

Man Of Style

In an age when so many sports heroes have fallen from grace, Tiger stands out from the pack, with his practically squeaky clean image. He was an "A" student at his California high school before enrolling at Stanford University. He loves his family. Perhaps this is part of the reason (along with his amazing talent, of course), that so many companies are eager to sign him to an endorsement deal. Alex Batchelor, the managing director of the consulting agency Interbrand, which specializes in brand marketing, said: "In a marketing context, Tiger Woods is a dream come true. He is articulate, intelligent, polite, courteous, mixed-race and a man at the top of his sport. He has a whole stack of personality positives that make him a hard act to beat." Batchelor, among many others, predicted that Tiger would likely become the first billionaire athlete.

Tiger's popularity is particularly interesting given his uneasy relationship with reporters. In 1997, a *GQ* profile revealed his proclivity for dirty jokes.

AP/WWP

Tiger shares his knowledge of the game with young golfers at the Tiger Woods Foundation Junior Golf Clinic in New Orleans.

That same year, the *National Enquirer* ran a tell-all story from his high school girlfriend, as well as a photo of him dancing with a voluptuous blonde under the headline "Tiger's Wild Night With Topless Dancer." "A lot of things they write are fabrications," he said. "Sensationalism sells: Don't let the facts get in the way of a good story. You have to understand that going in." Since then he has been known for being extremely closed during his rare one-on-one interviews and his other interactions with the media. Always polite, but always distant.

His Heritage

After Tiger won his first Masters in 1997, he appeared on *The Oprah Show* where he coined the term "Cablinasian" to describe his multi-ethnic heritage of Caucasion, Native American, African-American and Asian roots.

His way of doing things is completely different from other superstars of the sport. Arnold Palmer amped up the game's popularity in the 1960s by talking to fans and indulging writers. He always had time for journalists, knew all their names and bought them drinks.

Legendary golfer Arnold Palmer helped golf's popularity in the 1960s by putting himself in the public eye.

Tiger, however, subscribes to a completely different philosophy – yet it has not affected his popularity. In fact, it's interesting to note that the comments he made in the *GQ* article were pretty much dismissed by the public as a result of his youth. The press doesn't attack him in the way other sports stars are discussed, either. In 2000, he was heard cursing on television after a bad drive at the U.S. Open. He also filmed a commercial during the Screen Actors Guild strike, despite being a member of the organization. Neither of these actions have had any significant repercussions for him. Observers have noted that his extraordinary talents and widespread popularity have immunized him from the criticism to which other public figures are subjected.

The Best

Reporters prove they can't get enough of Tiger Woods at the practice for the 2001 Nissan Open.

Part of the reason that controversy does not seem to affect Tiger may be because he does not court it. His father has declared in the past that Tiger would be an instrument of social change, but Tiger seems to shy away from issues that would take the focus off his game. In a unique position to take some strong public stands, Tiger usually opts for diplomatic answers. His focus is always on golf. "I don't just want to be the best black player or the best Asian player," said Tiger. "I want to be the best golfer ever." Some may argue that at age 25, he already is.

2001: The Year Of The Tiger

Four-In-A-Row!
The 2001 Masters Victory

While much of the hype leading up to the 2001 Masters was focused on Tiger Woods and the controversy over whether or not he was in the running for a "Grand Slam," viewers of the tournament were treated to four days of drama, glory and a thrilling finish.

Tiger Woods came to the Augusta National Golf Club in April of 2001 with a heavy burden on his shoulders. Having won his past three majors, Tiger now had a chance to complete a fourth challenge. Conquering the Masters would give him victories in all four of the most recent major PGA tournaments – a task rarely achieved in the golfing world. A task that would become known as the "Tiger Slam."

The Competition

However, it was not going to be an easy battle. It became clear very early that Tiger was the one man everyone wanted to beat. And there was no shortage of competition hoping to finally give Tiger a run for his money.

Would this be the year for David Duval, who had come so close in three previous Masters, but had yet to slip his arms into the sleeves of the Green Jacket? Duval, whose wrist tendinitis caused him to miss several weeks of the 2001 tour, put a positive spin on his forced "vacation" from the sport. "If anything, one thing I have going for me is that I'm the freshest in the field," he joked.

Phil Mickelson waits with anticipation as his ball rolls toward the cup at the 18th hole at the 2001 Masters.

Perhaps Phil Mickelson, who had been successful in stopping the red-hot Tiger in the past, would find victory at Augusta. There was an entire field of worthy competitors, including Mark Calcavecchia, Fred Couples and the defending Masters champion, Vijay Singh. Each of these golfers could claim a legitimate opportunity to win the championship.

Day One: A Promising Start

The start of the 65th Masters Tournament was a shaky one for Tiger, who bogeyed on the first hole. But Tiger soon found his groove and began playing at a pace equal to the one he had set during his 1997 Masters victory.

Drama was supplied early in the tournament by Chris DiMarco, a 32-year-old rookie playing in his first Masters event. DiMarco's opening round score of 65 helped to place him in the unlikely position of being atop the tournament's leaderboard.

AP/WWP

Chris DiMarco shined in the first two rounds of the 2001 Masters.

But Tiger was never far behind. The golfing prodigy shot a 70 on his first day, placing him in a tie for 15th place. But he wasn't worried. The last time he shot a score this low in the first round at Augusta was in 1997 – the same year he won the Masters by an amazing 12 strokes.

"This is a major championship," he told the press after day one. "It's four days, and everyone knows it's awfully hard to go out and shoot in the mid-60s every day in a major."

Day Two: In Full Swing

DiMarco's surprising reign continued throughout the second day, as he shot a 69, giving him the Masters' rookie record of 134 after 36 holes. A number of recognizable names sat near the top of the scoreboard. Tournament favorites Duval and Mickelson were there – and so was Tiger.

In fact, at the conclusion of play on Friday, Duval was three shots off the lead, and only one shot back from Tiger and Mickelson, who were both tied in a fierce battle for second.

As always, there were several golfers who didn't make the cut after the first two days of the Masters. While legends Jack Nicklaus, Arnold Palmer and Gary Player (who shared a group for the second conseccutive year) weren't expected to

Tiger kicks in frustration as he misses a putt during the second round of the 2001 Masters.

competitively contend anymore, others such as Davis Love III and Greg Norman also missed the cut. Norman was particularly upset with his lackluster performance. "Ugly. One word. Now, I can go," said Norman, summing up his two days at Augusta.

Day Three: Tiger Takes The Lead

As the weekend began, Tiger proved to everyone that he wasn't ready to relinquish his chance at holding all four major titles at once. Many fans arrived at Augusta to see if Tiger could accomplish this seemingly impossible feat. But judging by the electricity in the crowd, the gallery was even more

Yipping No More

After Chris DiMarco's great performance at the 2001 Masters, it's hard to believe that he once considered quitting the sport. Golfer Skip Kendall remembers one grim tournament when, "[DiMarco] said, 'That's it, I'm done. I quit. I can't take it anymore. I've got the yips. I can't make it from a foot.'" Fortunately, no one held DiMarco to his promise.

Dave Cannon/AllSport

David Duval holds his swing as he watches his tee-off shot.

excited at the prospect of witnessing a tense match that came down to the wire. And as Day Three came to a close, it became obvious that the spectators would get their wish.

Phil Mickelson, the man who ended Tiger's six-tournament winning streak in February 2001 and perhaps Tiger's top competitor, stood just one shot down from Tiger's 4-under 204 total. David Duval, Mark Calcavecchia and Japan's Toshimitsu Izawa were not far behind. In fact, 12 players stood within five shots of the young leader.

Tiger acknowledged the fierce competition that would face him the next day. "I know that there are a lot of other good players at the top of the leaderboard who have a wonderful chance of winning [Sunday] if they just play a good, solid round," he said. "So I'm going to go out there with the intent of just trying to keep the ball in play and put it on the green so I have, hopefully, some uphill putts."

Day Four: Duval's Dreams Dashed

Day Four was filled with suspense as the lead changed hands from hole to hole. Duval, Mickelson and Tiger quickly separated themselves as the major contenders for the Green Jacket.

The fans gasped and cheered as their favorite players made their putts with precision and accuracy, keeping within just a few strokes of each other. "When you're shooting a good score and making a game out of this, [the fans] appreciate it. That's what makes this so special. They appreciate the show you put on here," said Duval. By birdieing six of the first eight holes, Duval stayed near the top of the pack, and even took sole possession of first place after the eighth hole.

Tiger and his trusty 8-iron kept most of the competition at arm's length throughout the tournament. It was on the 11th hole, with Mickelson nipping at his heels, that Tiger's 8-iron came close to sinking a hole-in-one from approximately 145 yards back. The 8-iron also served Tiger well on the 13th hole, when he used it to land the ball on the green and followed it with a two-putt birdie.

Vijay Singh relinquishes the coveted Masters title to Tiger Woods on April 8, 2001.

Amy Sancetta/AllSport

As the tournament entered its final 12 holes and approached the climactic back nine, Duval, Mickelson and Tiger seemed intent on providing a spectacular show. A picture-perfect birdie by Duval on the 15th hole put him in a tie with Tiger with only three holes left to play.

Unfortunately for Duval, this show had a particularly cruel ending. First, two missed opportunities, including a botched 8-foot putt, resulted in a bogey on the 16th hole. Missed putts on 17 and 18 followed. "I had a few opportunities coming home that I wish I could have capitalized on," he said. "I made my share of putts early, but I missed a few late."

Mickelson didn't fare much better down the stretch. Down by only one shot, he also bogeyed on the 16th hole, missing a putt from 8 feet, effectively placing him out of contention. Mickelson could only blame himself. "I needed to give myself a good birdie putt, and I didn't do it," he said.

King Of The Course

While the competition may have wilted when the heat was turned up, Tiger found one more occasion to shine in the tournament. His 18-foot birdie on the 18th hole clinched the Masters victory and capped off one of the most improbable title runs in the history of golf. "This is the greatest thing I've ever accomplished," Tiger said after his win. "You don't think about winning four majors in a row when you're a kid. All I ever dreamed about was competing against the best players and hopefully winning some majors. But four in a row? Yeah, I'm a little amazed."

His peers were equally awe-struck by Tiger's performance. "He's not like anyone we've seen before in this game," said Mark Calcavecchia. Even the legends of the sport have nothing but praise for the gifted youngster. Jack Nicklaus, who has more major victories under his belt than anybody who has ever played the game of golf, said, "What Tiger has done is the most remarkable feat, not only in golf but probably in all of sports."

Tiger appeared to be overcome by his emotions after his Masters victory. With both his mother and father by his side, Tiger wiped away tears of joy — the tears of a champion.

Tiger Food

Tiger, who shared a home with fellow golfer Mark O'Meara during the Masters, ate well during the tournament. In fact, the two men flew a personal chef in from London to prepare all of their meals!

The lion may be king of the forest, but Tiger rules the golf course. The young champion surveys the fairway with his caddie and trusted friend, Steve Williams.

AP/WWP

Tiger And The Grand Slam

Did he or didn't he? By holding all four major golf titles at once, Tiger Woods is the only modern-day golfer ever to accomplish such a feat. But is it truly a Grand Slam?

Even before Tiger won his fourth consecutive major tournament at the Masters in April 2001, the debate raged as to whether this incredible accomplishment could be considered a true Grand Slam – a legendary feat which has been largely discussed, but rarely approached, in golf over the past century.

"The Impregnable Quadrilateral"

Bobby Jones was the first golfer to win a Grand Slam. It occurred in 1930, when the four greatest events on the golf calendar were the British Amateur, British Open, U.S. Amateur and U.S. Open tournaments. Jones' feat was initially called "The Impregnable Quadrilateral," but later took on the easier to pronounce title of "Grand Slam."

The modern-era Grand Slam refers to winning all four major PGA events (the U.S. Open, the British Open, the Masters and the PGA Championship) in the same calendar year. The modern Slam originated when Arnold Palmer and *Pittsburgh Press* reporter Bob Drum shared a flight to the 1960 British Open. Palmer remembers, "I said: 'Gee, Bob, wouldn't it be great if I would win the British Open, come back . . . and win the PGA?'"

The grandchildren of Bobby Jones unveil a stamp that commemorates Jones' 1930 Grand Slam.

Palmer ultimately failed in his attempt at the Slam, as have all the other golfers who have followed in his quest. Winning the Grand Slam is an honor that eluded even Jack Nicklaus, and it's that very elusiveness that has elevated the modern-day "Grand Slam" to its exalted status in golf lore. Although no golfer has ever won the Masters, PGA Championship, U.S. Open and British Open in the same season, Tiger Woods became only the fifth golfer to join the ranks of golfers who have scored a "career" Grand Slam in July 2000 with his win at the British Open. And, with his April 2001 Masters win, Tiger is the only golfer to hold all four major titles at the same time. The legendary few who have won each of the four events over the course of their career also include Ben Hogan, Jack Nicklaus, Gary Player and Gene Sarazen.

"No way, Jose"

Tiger's 2001 Masters win capped off a flurry of debate as to whether it was a true Grand Slam or not. Asked before Tiger's Masters victory, Arnold Palmer responded, "No way, Jose." He then elaborated on his comments, saying, "You've got to win all four in one year. That doesn't take a thing away from him – but it don't cut any beans with me."

Many other golf legends have agreed with Palmer. Gary Player believes Tiger lost his chance at the Slam when he didn't win the 2000 Masters. "Who won the Masters last year? Vijay Singh. Tiger Woods had the chance then, didn't he?" said Player.

Sam Snead agrees, saying, "You've got to do it in the same year. That's what it has always been." Jack Nicklaus released a statement on his website, which

Gary Player, shown here at the 2000 British Open, said Tiger's run shouldn't qualify as a Grand Slam.

reads, "The question keeps being asked of me: Is it a Grand Slam? I don't think it makes a difference. By the definition of a Grand Slam, no it's not. But, what it's called is irrelevant."

Nicklaus might not know what to call Tiger's feat, but his appropriate suggestion, the "Fiscal Slam," has been jokingly considered. Others, including several members of the press, have fittingly referred to the incident as the "Tiger Slam."

The Ghost Of Mr. Jones

In response to questions about what he would say to golf legend Bobby Jones about the Grand Slam, Tiger has answered, "First question I'd probably ask him: 'What the heck are you doing here?'"

A few contemporary golfers have sided with the legends in the great debate. Steve Strickler says, "I just don't think it's a Grand Slam because he didn't do it all in one year." David Duval echoes these sentiments, saying, "As much as I'd like for it to be thought of that way, I don't think you could look back on it 50 years from now and say that it was."

Slam Supporters

While there are some dissenters, most of today's professional players seem to disagree with their elders on the matter. Mark Calcavecchia has said, "I'd say it's a Grand Slam. I know some of the historians feel differently. They think you need to win all four in one year."

"[Tiger's] got four [trophies] together on the mantle right now, and that's a Grand Slam. It doesn't matter what order it came in," added rookie golfer Chris DiMarco.

Tiger celebrates after sinking an eagle putt to defeat Vijay Singh at 2000's Grand Slam of Golf.

APWWP

Nick Price is another player who agrees with the mantle theory. "I mean, it's not officially a Grand Slam, because it's not done in a calendar year, but if you've got possession of all four of those trophies at one time, it's a Slam. Don't they say possession is nine-tenths of the law?"

Tiger even has the support of one of the most important men in golf. PGA Tour commissioner Tim Finchem says, "I think it's a Slam, with all due respect to Jack and Arnie."

One person who has tried to stay above the fray is Tiger Woods. He prefers to let others decide what to call it. "I don't think it's right for me to comment on that," said Tiger about the ongoing debate. "But it will probably go down as one of the top moments in our sport."

Tiger Talks

When asked about how it felt to join the ranks of golfers who have won a Grand Slam, such as Gary Player and Jack Nicklaus, Tiger said, "Those are true champions right there. Every one is a true champion." He then went on to add, "They have been the cream of the crop. They've been the elite players, not only during their time, but ever to play the game. To be in the same breath as those guys makes it very special. "

Although Tiger didn't win all four events in a single calendar year stretching from January to December, he still won all four events in the span of 294 days, which places him well under the 365 days in a calendar year. And who says Tiger's finished yet? At the rate Tiger is going, he may yet complete that "official" Grand Slam before his career is over.

AP/WWP

After winning the Masters in 2001, Tiger quickly found his way to his father, Earl, and shared an emotional moment.

Prelude To Victory

"Each and every year that I've played golf, I've become better," said Tiger Woods at the start of the 2001 season. Many thought that the year 2000 would be a hard act to follow. However, now that Tiger's hit his stride, it looks like he's prepared to surpass his past achievements and set yet another new standard in golf. Here's a look at Tiger's 2001 season leading up to his historic victory at the Masters.

At first, it may have looked like it wouldn't happen. Starting painfully slow, Tiger went without a single win for his first five PGA tournaments of the year, causing many people to wonder if maybe Tiger's tremendous success had finally run its course. But Tiger knew otherwise. And two impressive victories – including a win at THE PLAYERS Championship – proved him right, and assured the world that Tiger's reign as golf's #1 son was anything but over.

Tiger eyeballs his shot at the 2001 Mercedes Championship.

AP/WWP

Mercedes Championship

(Jan. 8-14)

The warm winds tearing across Hawaii on the tournament's opening day didn't exactly make things easy for anyone. And certainly they didn't help Tiger's performance in the first round. At the ninth hole, Tiger sent his ball so far out of bounds that he almost couldn't find it. When the tournament was over, Tiger found himself tied for seventh place with Michael Clark II, Justin Leonard and David Toms, at 12 under par.

Phoenix Open (Jan. 22-28)

When Tiger first teed up in Phoenix, things seemed to be going much better for him. He would eventually finish the first round with a 6-under-par 65, and may have scored even higher if it hadn't been for the orange that was hurled toward him at the ninth hole. Police would later detain a 15-year-old boy, who claimed that he had thrown the orange on a dare. The next round wasn't so impressive and Mark Calcavecchia eventually took home the prize. Tiger's score of 13 under par tied Chris DiMarco for fifth place.

Saved By The Neck

A fan inadvertently helped Tiger win the Bay Hill Invitational, just by being there! At the 18th hole in the fourth round, Tiger's shot was headed out of bounds when it hit a spectator in the neck and bounced to the ground, remaining on the course and in play.

AT&T Pebble Beach National Pro-Am

(Jan. 29-Feb. 4)

Although Tiger's game at Pebble Beach was literally not up to par, it wasn't exactly his fault. Just before the tournament, Tiger was signing autographs when one fan lunged ahead of the others. Tiger accidentally stepped on the fan's ankle – hyperextending his knee – and was diagnosed with a sprained ligament. Tiger was still able to score an impressive eight birdies in the first round, however. But he wasn't able to make the grade against the eventual winner Davis Love III, and finished up tied for eighth place.

Buick Invitational (Feb. 5-11)

With his hair back to its original color (after a brief "experiment" as a blond), Tiger was able to shoot 17 under par at the Buick Invitational. He came in fourth place behind a three-way tie for first, from which Phil Mickelson emerged the victor.

Nissan Open (Feb. 19-25)

Despite his best efforts, Tiger wasn't able to play up to his usual standards at the Nissan Open. Finishing the second round only four strokes behind leaders Miguel Angel Jiminez and Davis Love III put him on a good track, but he wasn't able to keep up and barely made par in the fourth round. While Robert Allenby took home the victory, Tiger ended up tied for 13th place.

Dubai Desert Classic (Mar. 1-4)

In the midst of a less-than-perfect season, Tiger decided to try his hand on foreign soil. For the Dubai Desert Classic, an international tournament not affiliated with the PGA Tour, he traveled all the way to the United Arab Emirates. Tiger and Thomas Bjorn were neck-and-neck for most of the tour, with Tiger usually ending the day ahead. In fact, Tiger probably would have come home with his first victory of 2001 if his ball hadn't ended up in the water on the very last hole in the fourth round!

Bay Hill Invitational (Mar. 12-18)

Tournament host Arnold Palmer helps Tiger into his jacket for winning the 2001 Bay Hill Invitational – his first win of the year.

Tiger beat his old rival Phil Mickelson by a single stroke at Bay Hill to finally break out of his dry spell and emerge the winner! Oddly enough, Tiger attributed his Bay Hill success to luck. "You're going to have to somehow grab some great breaks and have luck on your side." Whether it was because of luck or skill, it was time for him to be back where he belonged – on top.

THE PLAYERS Championship (Mar. 19-25)

It was a hard battle against Vijay Singh in THE PLAYERS Championship, but Tiger's 5-under-par score of 67 on the last day put him over the top and in the winning position. When Singh missed the birdie on the tournament's very last hole, Tiger was able to take the title with a bogey.

The Makings Of
A Grand Slam

The Masters

Arguably the most famous tournament in the United States, the Masters has been creating memories and crowning champions since 1934. Based at the Augusta National Golf Club in Augusta, Georgia, the Masters (along with its legendary Green Jacket) holds a special place in the hearts of golf fans everywhere.

The youngest of the four modern Grand Slam events, the Masters certainly had the right pedigree to succeed. Established by banker Clifford Roberts and golfing great Bobby Jones, who wanted to organize an annual tournament in his home state of Georgia, the Masters was launched in 1934 as the Augusta National Invitation Tournament.

Bobby Jones takes a practice swing.

Held on March 22, 1934, the first tournament was a huge success, drawing top talent like Jones – who had retired in 1930 but was persuaded by Club members to join the field – Craig Wood and Walter Hagen. Horton Smith took first place and $1,500, finishing one stroke ahead of Wood. Smith would also become the first two-time Masters winner in 1936.

The tournament underwent some changes over the next few years, most importantly in regard to its name. Almost from the start, Bobby Jones was pressured to rename the event the Masters, which he thought was too pretentious. But in 1939, Jones relented, and the tournament took its now-familiar name. Another change came the next year, when the tournament's date was moved from March to the first full week of April.

Hulton Deutsch/Allsport

Playing The Masters

Some of the unique, beautiful and quirky features of the Masters' home course at Augusta include:

■ Magnolia Lane – a glorious, 250-yard long path lined with 61 Magnolia trees, planted in the late 1850s.

■ "Amen Corner" – holes 11, 12 and 13 were named by sportswriter Herbert Warren Wind to describe Arnold Palmer's spectacular feats en-route to his 1958 Masters win.

Nice Threads!

The great tradition of the Green Jacket had a very modest start. In 1937, the club asked its members to wear the distinctive (and unpopular) jackets so that visitors would know who to go to for information. But in 1949, the jacket took a very different role when it was placed on the powerful shoulders of 'Slammin' Sam Snead to commemorate his Masters victory.

Today, the Green Jacket is one of the most famous sports symbols in the world. As the tournament draws to a close, several jackets are prepared to suit the leading players (and potential winner) for the ceremony. Afterward, the winner's measurements are taken and a custom jacket is made for him, so he can "style and profile" until the next Masters.

Another great Masters tradition, the Champions Dinner, got its start in 1952. The dinner is held the Tuesday before the tournament for all previous Masters winners. The defending champion serves as the host and has the heavy responsibility of choosing the menu!

Augusta National

One of the most beautiful courses in the world, Augusta National has hosted every Masters tournament since its inception. The course was designed by Bobby Jones and Scottish designer Dr. Alister Mackenzie and opened in 1932

The Eisenhower Tree

Commonly referred to as "The Eisenhower Tree;" a 65-foot tree on the 17th hole was named for club member, President Dwight Eisenhower. Apparently, Eisenhower hit the tree so often he actually requested it be cut down (thankfully, it wasn't!).

on a plot of land that was originally used as a plant nursery. Many of the flora that grace the grounds are the legacy of the course's days as a nursery. In fact, every hole on the course is named after a tree, plant or flower found near it (e.g., Golden Bell, Holly and Tea Olive).

Great Masters Moments

Through the years, Masters fans have witnessed some of the greatest moments in all of golf:

In 1935, Gene Sarazen was trailing front-runner Craig Wood by three strokes after his first shot at the par-5 15th hole. But Sarazen came back with an incredible second shot. Officially a 220-yard shot (Sarazen later claimed it went 232 or 235 yards), Sarazen's double eagle tied him with Wood (whom he would beat in a playoff) and is known as "the shot heard 'round the world."

Byron Nelson and Ben Hogan starred in a memorable Masters in 1942. Tied after regulation play, the two legends squared off in an amazing 18-hole playoff that kept fans riveted. The battle went Nelson's way, thanks to an 11-hole stretch of 6-under par, and Nelson edged Hogan by one shot, 69 to 70.

Jack Nicklaus has been involved in two great Masters moments. In 1975, he survived a three-man dogfight against Tom Weiskopf and Johnny Miller by sinking an incredible 40-foot birdie putt on the 16th. Eleven years later, amidst questions about retirement, Nicklaus silenced his critics and became, at age 46, the oldest Masters winner – with a little help from a Greg Norman bogey at the 18th and a blown 12-foot putt by Tom Kite.

Veteran Larry Mize put a dramatic stamp on a great 1987 Masters. He entered a sudden-death playoff battle with Seve Ballesteros (who was eliminated after the first hole) and Greg Norman. Mize's shot at the second hole put him about 140 feet from the cup, while Norman enjoyed a better position just on the green. With little more than a prayer, Mize bounced a chip shot onto the green that – amazingly – rolled right into the cup! Norman missed his putt, leaving Mize the winner, thanks to that amazing shot.

Ben Hogan (left) poses with winner Byron Nelson at the 1942 Masters.

AP/WWP

Different emotions carried the day at the 1995 Masters. In addition to missing the cut in three of his last four events, Ben Crenshaw went into the Masters only two days after the funeral of his longtime mentor, Harvey Penick. It would have been easy for Crenshaw to fold, but he played tough and was locked in a tie after 16 holes. But he pulled away late, and when his final putt dropped on the 18th, Crenshaw provided an unforgettable moment by doubling over and covering his face with his hands, overcome with the joy of a Masters win that he would dedicate to his friend.

Tiger At The Masters

Though Tiger Woods has enjoyed his own Masters moments, it didn't look like he would ever tame the course after his first two cracks at Augusta National. In 1995, he finished tied for a lowly 41st place, finishing at 5 over par. Things got worse in 1996, when Tiger failed to make the cut after the first two rounds.

Obviously, he learned something! Tiger came roaring back in the 1997 Masters, putting together a record-setting tournament. He not only destroyed the field by winning the tournament by 12 strokes, but he also became the youngest Masters champion in history at the age of 21. His score of 270 beat the record set by Jack Nicklaus in 1965 and tied by Ray Floyd in 1976. When all was said and done, Tiger had set 20 tournament records and tied six others in one of the greatest golf performances in history.

AP/WWP

The Masters would also become the setting for Tiger's historic fourth consecutive major title in 2001. (For a look at Tiger's 2001 Masters win, see *Four-In-A-Row! The 2001 Masters* on page 17).

Tiger Woods celebrates his incredible record-breaking win at the 1997 Masters.

The U.S. Open

With over 100 years of impressive history under its belt, the U.S. Open continues to be a favorite of professionals, fans and amateurs alike.

The United States Golf Association (USGA) was formed in 1894 to regulate national golf standards and established the U.S. Amateur tournament – a tournament which would become the premier amateur golfing event in the country – in 1895. Since amateur golfers were more respected than professionals at the time, the one-day event for professionals scheduled for the following day was merely an afterthought. But that exhibition tournament would eventually grow into the well-respected U.S. Open that we know today.

Theodore Havemeyer's backing (and his country club) made the U.S. Open possible.

That first professional exhibition tournament took place on October 4, 1895 in Newport, Rhode Island hardly surprising, as the owner of the Newport Golf and Country Club, Theodore Havemeyer, was also the first president of the USGA! The event was a 36-hole affair (four rounds of nine holes) which drew only 11 players, one of whom was an amateur. English pro Horace Rawlins took the first Open title with a score of 173. His take was $150 in cash (a good haul, by 1895 standards), a gold medal and ownership of the Open Championship Cup for a year.

In 1898, the Open went solo by taking place on a different course than the U.S. Amateur for the first time. Also that year, the Open expanded to three days and 72 holes (with 36 played on the last day). This format would last until 1965, when the event moved to its current four-day, 72-hole format.

For much of its early years, the Open was seen as an "ugly sister" to the Amateur. That changed in 1913 when American Francis Ouimet defeated English players Harry Vardon and Ted Ray in a playoff. This helped popularize the tournament and sparked interest in golf all over the country. Amateur Bobby Jones also gave the Open some publicity with his four career wins (including his Grand Slam campaign in 1930). Sam Snead, Ben Hogan, Jack Nicklaus and now Tiger Woods have all turned in memorable U.S. Open performances and helped turn a fledgling tournament into one of the four premier events in the country.

In The Words Of A Winner

In 1951, Ben Hogan celebrated the third of his four U.S. Open wins. The course, Oakland Hills in Michigan, had been modified to make play harder and the tough terrain had really tested his abilities. While accepting the tournament trophy, Hogan said "I am glad I brought this course, this monster, to its knees."

Wide Open

Yes, even *you* can play in the U.S. Open – if you have a handicap of 1.4 or better, and you're one of the lucky folks to make the cut at a USGA 18-hole qualifying tournament. Then you'll have to make another cut at a 36-hole tournament held two weeks before the Open.

The Open is played at a different course each year, although notable locations like Pebble Beach and the Olympic Club have hosted it more than once. The kicker – and the bane of many golfers – is that Open courses are modified to make them more difficult. Changes include narrowing the fairways and shortening par-5s to long par-4s.

Great U.S. Open Moments

In the 1919 U.S. Open, golfing great and flamboyant socialite Walter Hagen put his legendary stature to the test. Trailing Mike Brady on the eve

The Trophy

The first Open Championship Cup was destroyed by a fire in 1946 at the Tam O'Shanter Country Club in Chicago. A second was made for 1947, and a copy of this trophy is presented to the tournament winner.

of the final round, Hagen reportedly spent the entire night at a party hosted by entertainer Al Jolson. After a quick shower the next morning, Hagen not only finished the grueling 36-hole round, but beat Brady by one stroke for the win.

In another memorable Open moment, just 16 months after a near-fatal car accident, Ben Hogan was struggling to regain his form at the 1950 Open. Despite some tough times, an amazing shot on the 18th hole helped Hogan force a three-way playoff the next day. The rejuvenated Hogan saved his best plays of the day for last, winning the playoff by a single stroke – but also partly due to opponent Lloyd Mangrum's two-stroke penalty for picking up his golf ball to brush off a bug!

Hogan's luck wasn't quite as good at the 1955 U.S. Open. All but declared the winner of the tournament, Hogan was relaxing in the clubhouse when he learned that obscure golfer Jack Fleck made two birdies

Legend-beater Jack Fleck warms up for his playoff against Ben Hogan in the 1955 U.S. Open.

and two pars on the last four holes to tie him. In the playoff the next day, Hogan slipped while driving on the 18th and drove the ball into a hay pile. Hogan couldn't recover, and Fleck took the playoff for the victory.

Ken Venturi's courageous 1964 Open performance might be the greatest effort in tournament history. Battling a humid 100-degree day and chronic back and neck injuries, Venturi played the 36-hole final round against the advice of a doctor. Struggling through torrid conditions, Venturi came back from a two-stroke deficit to beat the field by a commanding four strokes.

While fending off late challenges by Arnold Palmer and Bruce Campton at the 1972 Open, Jack Nicklaus made one of the luckiest shots in golf history. Facing a brutal wind on the 17th hole, Nicklaus altered his stroke in mid-swing, sending the ball sailing through the wind and off the flagstick! The ball rested inches from the cup – close enough for a birdie putt and the win.

Another memorable shot came from veteran Tom Watson in 1987. After a neck-and-neck tournament, Watson went to the 18th hole tied with the unheralded Scott Simpson. Watson had to make a treacherous uphill, 45-foot putt to maintain the tie. The shot was on-line – but stopped just inches short of the cup, giving Simpson an unexpected win.

The 2000 U.S. Open at Pebble Beach was a memorable event not only for Tiger Woods' record-breaking performance, but the emotional and touching tribute to Payne Stewart. Stewart had died in a plane crash only four months after winning the Open the previous year. In honor of their fallen comrade, some 40 golfers lined up to hit balls into the ocean. It was a fitting salute to the 1999 Open champion who never had the chance to defend his title.

Tiger At The U.S. Open

It took Tiger Woods a few years to polish his style for the U.S. Open. A wrist injury kept him out in 1995 and he probably wished the same had happened in 1996, when he finished with a 294 and tied for 82nd place. His uninspiring 19th-place finish in 1997 (his first U.S. Open as a pro) didn't help, either. And when Tiger finished 10 over par in 1998, the frustration must have been great. But by 1999, Tiger's Open fortunes seemed to turn, as he tied for third with a 281.

After rewriting the record books at the 100th U.S. Open in 2000, Tiger celebrates with his mom.

That set the stage for one of the most incredible performances of his young career in the 2000 Open at Pebble Beach. Tiger put the competition away early. Second place finisher Ernie Els spoke for all of Tiger's victims when he remarked "I could have played out of my mind and still lost by six or seven." Tiger won by a shocking 15 strokes – the largest margin of victory in a major since 1862! When the dust settled, Tiger had set or tied 10 tournament records en route to the first of four consecutive major victories.

The British Open

Throughout the years, many people have felt that no other tournament has the heritage and tradition of the British Open. With its long history of great champions, classic courses and rivalry between European and American players and fans, the British Open has delighted audiences for nearly 150 years.

The world's oldest golf championship can trace its roots back to the ancestral home of golf itself. In 1856, members of the Prestwick Golf Club in Ayrshire, Scotland, met to organize an annual tournament to crown a golfing champion. But it was another four years before the Ayrshire club took the plunge and held the first British Open on October 17, 1860.

Eight players took part in that first tourney, a one-day event of 36 holes (three rounds of 12 holes each). Willie Park's winning score of 174 won him the Championship Belt, a prize to be presented to each year's champion. If a player won three British Opens in a row, he would be awarded the belt permanently.

No one ruled the early British Opens like Old Tom Morris – except his son!

APWWP

Imagine the surprise when Tom Morris Jr. won his third consecutive Open in 1870! It wasn't the only time the Morris family terrorized the Open. Both Old Tom and Tom Jr. dominated with eight Open titles between them by 1872. For that year's Open, the committee introduced the Claret Jug as the prize – the same prize that is awarded today.

Also in 1872, the British Open began rotating among different golf courses in

Scotland, and was held in England for the first time in 1892. The tournament's success attracted more golfers and, in 1892, resulted in the expansion of the event to 72 holes over two days.

Some of golf's greatest players found success at the British Open, including Harry Vardon (6 wins), James Braid (5 wins), Walter Hagen (4 wins) and Bobby Jones (3 wins). When the tournament resumed after World War II, many American players shunned it until the prize money was increased in 1960. That encouraged players like Arnold Palmer, Jack Nicklaus, Lee Trevino and Tom Watson to cross the Atlantic and take a shot at the British Open. Many European fans bemoaned the American dominance of the tournament until the 1980s, when European players like Seve Ballesteros, Nick Faldo and Sandy Lyle won the coveted Claret Jug.

Who, What And Where?

AP/WWP

Any amateur or pro who makes the cut by playing in two different qualifying rounds can have a chance at participating in the British Open. The Open has been held on many of Great Britain's oldest and most famous courses, such as Royal Lytham, Turnberry and St. Andrews.

Nick Faldo, who has won the British Open, is seen here practicing at Royal Lytham St. Annes.

Great British Open Moments

Royal Lytham St. Annes Golf Club provided a great moment in 1926, thanks to Bobby Jones' sweet swing. Tied for the lead and stuck in a bunker on the 17th hole, Jones needed a miracle to keep him in the game. After his 175-yard drive dropped in and won him the Open, the Royal Lytham commemorated Jones' feat with a plaque on the 17th hole and a display of his iron.

In 1972, Lee Trevino would hit a stunning shot of his own and deny Jack Nicklaus a piece of history. Nicklaus was trying to join Ben Hogan as the only player to win the Masters, U.S. Open and British Open in one year. Nicklaus had a tough late-hole stretch and found himself one stroke behind Trevino. To keep ahead of Nicklaus, Trevino needed to

International Rivalry

As the only major played outside the U.S. and the oldest tournament in the world, national pride takes center stage at the British Open. The British Open's record of American vs. European winners gets a lot of ink come tournament time. Maybe it's not always healthy, but it's sure a lot of fun!

sink a chip shot out of the rough. When he hacked with his 9-iron and rolled the ball right in the cup, Trevino won and derailed Nicklaus' historic effort.

Another amazing shot decided the 1994 British Open, this time off the putter of Nick Price. Trailing Jesper Parnevik on the 17th hole, Price found himself 50 feet from the cup. With nerves of steel, Price stroked an amazing putt for an eagle that put the pressure squarely on Parnevik, who bogeyed on 18 to give Price the win. The putt capped an amazing tournament for Price, who shot in the 60s in all four rounds.

Although Constantino Rocca lost the 1995 British Open in a playoff with John Daly, the Italian player provided one of the most emotional scenes in Open history. Thinking he was out for good after missing a putt, Rocca sunk a miraculous 60-foot birdie putt on the 18th to force an overtime session. Tears streaming down his face, Rocca sunk to his knees and pounded the turf as the crowd roared. Rocca eventually had to settle for second place, but what an unforgettable moment!

Rocca celebrates his amazing 18th hole putt in 1995.

AP/WWP

The 1999 British Open also offered what may be golf's worst "great moment" ever! Leading by three strokes going into the final hole, Jean Van de Velde suffered a horrendous sequence, landing in the bunker, the rough and a creek before taking a triple bogey! Van de Velde suddenly found himself in a three-way playoff with Justin Leonard and Paul Lawrie, who had roared back from a 10-stroke deficit. Lawrie easily beat both Leonard and Van de Velde for an unexpected Open win.

A Rose By Any Other Name

St. Andrews hasn't always been popular with players. Its rough terrain and often brutal winds can wreak havoc with players used to landscaped American courses. When Sam Snead first saw the Old Course in 1946 while traveling by train, he asked the man next to him "What abandoned golf course is that?"

Tiger At The British Open

Although Tiger has had better British Open luck than Van de Velde, it took a few tries for him hold his own. As an amateur in 1995 and 1996, he finished tied for 68th and 22nd, respectively. As a pro in 1997, he tied for 24th. His 1998 performance saw him shoot 1 over par and end up third. A tough 1999 tournament had him tied for 7th at ten over par.

AP/WWP

Tiger celebrates his 2000 British Open victory by kissing the Claret Jug.

Then came the 2000 British Open at St. Andrews. One month after blowing away the field in the U.S. Open, Tiger thundered into the British Open, winning with a colossal 19-under-par 269 and breaking Nick Faldo's tournament record set in 1990. The win also netted Tiger a career Grand Slam, making him the first to achieve the feat since Jack Nicklaus won his third in 1978. With that win, Tiger became the youngest career Grand Slam winner; the first player since Tom Watson in 1982 to win both the U.S. and British Open in the same year; and only the second player to win three major championships in the same year.

The PGA Championship

Since it first began in 1916, the PGA Championship has fulfilled the dreams of many golfers – and broken the hearts of others.

Like the PGA itself, the PGA Championship was the brainstorm of Rodman Wanamaker, who desired an annual match-play tournament (a tournament, often played in teams of two, in which the winner is determined by the most number of holes won) to determine a golfing champion. To achieve this goal, Wanamaker put up not only the $2,580 purse, but also commissioned the championship trophy that still bears his name.

The first PGA Championship tournament took place in 1916 at the Siwanoy Country Club in Bronxville, New York, where Jim Barnes took home the first trophy. After a two-year hiatus during World War I, the tournament returned in 1919, with Barnes winning again.

Moving Toward The Future

Over the next 30 years, some of the game's greatest players would excel in the PGA's big event. Walter Hagen won five championships in the 1920s, while Gene Sarazen won three. Byron Nelson appeared in the finals for five straight years. After the tournament was put on hold during World War II, Ben Hogan, Sam Snead and Doug Ford had great tournament runs of their own.

In 1958, faced with the reality that television was here to stay, the PGA abandoned match play for

APWWP

During the 1920s, pros like Walter Hagen (second from right) and Gene Sarazen (far right) won the PGA Championship.

the more television-friendly system of stroke play. The days of repeat champions were over. Since then, Tiger Woods has been the only player to win the Wanamaker Trophy two years in a row.

Courses And Currents

Unlike most tournaments, the PGA Championship is a professionals-only event. But the venue changes each year and it's been held at courses all over the country, from Pebble Beach to the Winged Foot Golf Club in Mamaroneck, New York. The 2001 PGA Championship will be held August 13-19 at the Atlantic Athletic Club in Duluth, Georgia.

PGA Championship Trivia

■ Tiger Woods is the only player to have won two consecutive PGA Championships since 1937 (1999 and 2000). He also has the lowest score under par, at -18 in 2000.

■ Walter Hagen and Jack Nicklaus are tied for the most PGA Championships; each golfer has won five times.

■ Colin Montgomerie and Steve Elkington share the record for the lowest total score in the Championship, with 267.

AP/WWP

Golf veteran Don January almost won the Wanamaker Trophy in 1961 before losing to Jerry Barber.

Great PGA Championship Moments

The greatest trio of shots in tournament play might have been at the 1961 PGA Championship at Olympia Fields in Illinois. On a 36-hole day (thanks to a second-round rain delay), Jerry Barber found himself four strokes behind Don January with three holes left to go. Undaunted, Barber sunk a 30-foot birdie putt on 16, a 40-foot par on 17, and an astounding 60-foot birdie putt on 18 to tie January and force an 18-hole playoff the next day. Barber fell behind early in the extra round, but roared back to take a one stroke victory.

The PGA was the only major to elude Arnold Palmer in his storied career, but he had a good shot at it in 1968. Under the brutal August sun, Palmer trailed Julius Boros by a stroke on the 18th hole. Palmer took the lead with a tremendous 3-wood shot to get on the green – then missed the putt! Boros' great chip shot sealed his victory and made the 48-year-old golfer the oldest PGA winner.

The 1986 PGA tournament saw Greg Norman up four strokes before faltering down the stretch. This gave underdog Bob Tway room to work some magic. Tway's approach on the 18th fairway landed right in the bunker. Trying only to get onto the green, Tway hit a bunker shot that rolled right into the cup for a stunning, tournament-winning birdie!

Tiger At The PGA Championship

After two uninspiring PGA finishes, Tiger finally broke through with his first PGA Championship in 1999 – but it wasn't easy! Tiger won by a single shot over 19-year-old Sergio Garcia, who missed two birdies on the last two holes.

In the 2000 PGA, Tiger was pushed to the limit by the then-unknown Bob May. Tied with May going into the 18th hole, Woods sunk a 6-foot birdie putt to force a three-hole playoff. The playoff went Tiger's way when a bad drive forced May to need to sink a 30-foot putt that came up just short. A triumphant Tiger later said, "It was a memorable battle today, and I enjoyed it. Birdie for birdie, shot for shot, we were going right at each other."

Tiger embraces opponent Bob May after winning the PGA Championship in 2000.

AP/WWP

The
Man

Tiger's Story

A decade ago, Eldrick "Tiger" Woods was a rising black golf star, a kid remarkable in the golfing world as much for his color as for his early amateur success. The young golfer often told reporters that one day he wanted to be not the best black player, but rather the best player, period. Today, at only age 25, Tiger is exactly that.

Tiger Woods is a superstar. He has brought golf to a whole new level, shaking up its long history of elitism and, in the process, attracting a new group of fans to the sport. He may be only 25 years old, but he has already lived a rich life filled with fame, success and the love of the family that means everything to him.

A Tiger Is Born

The nickname, "Tiger," wasn't just pulled out of the family hat; it was chosen long before Eldrick "Tiger" Woods was born on December 30, 1975 in the small, Southern California town of Cypress, years before anyone knew he'd be breaking long-standing golf records on his way to trophy after trophy. However, Eldrick's seemingly prophetic nickname, "Tiger," is now synonymous with the man who has conquered racial barriers, redefined a sport, and strikes fear in the heart of his fellow golfers.

Young Earl Woods didn't yet have a son when he fought in the Vietnam War as a Green Beret. What he did have was a best buddy

Tiger and a "friend" pose for a 1998 photo.

Heinz Kluetmeier/TimePix

named Vuong Dang Phong, who served as a soldier in the South Vietnamese Army. The men, both lieutenant colonels, watched each other's backs, shared miraculous escapes, and time after time risked their own lives to save the other. Phong was, Earl said later, the sole reason he came back to the United States alive. Phong was such a fearless fighter that Earl nicknamed him "Tiger."

Woody and Tiger, as the pair were known, were inseparable both on and off the battlefield. Both avid tennis players, they'd compete mightily during down times, then dress and run for the choppers when duty called, trading friendly competition for life-and-death cooperation. And when, tragically, Tiger went missing in action, Earl vowed that one day he himself would have a son, a fearless boy, and that boy would be named after his friend. Phong never was found, but his nickname lives on, and every time the name Tiger Woods appears in print, a little bit of honor accrues to the memory of the man who preserved his father's life.

Family Values

Honor and tradition are big parts of the Woods family's universe. While others consider it a great compliment to compare Tiger to Jack Nicklaus and Arnold Palmer, he himself says he admires those men for their golf, but doesn't consider them heroes. His father Earl, Tiger says, is his real role model, and he admires both his parents for teaching him respect for his ethnic heritage, among many, many other things.

Half of that heritage is Thai. Tiger's mother Kultida "Tida" Woods met Earl Woods while she was working in Bangkok, Thailand, as

Ken Levine/Allsport

The Woods family in 1990 – Tiger, his father, Earl and mother, Kultida, spend an afternoon on the golf course.

a secretary. Tiger's mom made it her business to raise a child of whom to be proud. She instructed him in the ways of Buddhism, avoided leaving him with baby sitters, and from the outset, taught him not to throw tantrums on the golf course. "I will not have a spoiled child," she would say, and referred to tennis players Jimmy Connors and John McEnroe as examples of bad sportsmanship. Golf, she told her son, was a gentleman's game, and although he should play to win, he should also be gracious and kind at all times. (Wonder what she thought when, on one occasion, she saw her toddler pulling down his pants, peeing in the sandtrap, and then resuming his game?)

Mom In The LPGA?

Earl wasn't the only proud parent out on the golf course playing the links with the young boy. According to Tiger, "[M]y mom played until I was about 10 and I started beating her regularly!" Even though Tiger ruled the green, his mom was still the authority when it came time to enforce the "house rules" of work before play.

For Earl's part, he hoped that his son would transform the golfing world so that a black man's place at the country club was not limited to the kitchen or the caddie shack. When Earl practiced his own golf swing with his infant son watching, he hoped to prove by example that golf was a game for all people, of all colors. At just 9 months old, barely able to walk, little Tiger took his first golf swing – complete with the pre-shot tushie wiggle – and Earl was the proudest daddy alive.

Child Prodigy

Hole-In-One

"I made my first hole-in-one when I was 8," Tiger recalls. "It was a 120-yard par-3, which I hit with my driver. Unfortunately, I was too short to see it go in, but when we heard all the yelling, my partner held me up to see that there was no ball on the green!"

Tiger entered his first tournament at age 3, but he was already a seasoned player by then. He and his dad were regular players at the Navy Golf Club in Cypress, where Tiger had, at age 3, shot an amazing score of 48 for nine holes in the kiddie competition. He'd been featured on *CBS News*, and even putted with Bob Hope on the *Mike Douglas Show*.

Major news shows from all around the country invited the young golf prodigy for interviews and demonstrations, and his elementary school years

DuomoCORBIS

Tiger waits for the ball to drop during the 1991 Junior Amateur Championship.

were marked by one junior championship win after another. Tiger wasn't a hotshot on the baseball diamond or a high-flying basketball star. He was the black kid with the unbeatable golf swing, the one who'd been trained by his father to be one of the best golfers in America. While most minority children were learning basketball or football from infancy, Earl said, his son was conquering the white man's game.

And "conquering" was a good word for it, because Tiger's training often resembled a battle. Using self-termed "psychological warfare," Earl bombarded Tiger with distractions at each hole – rolling balls across his path and making noises or side comments – in order to teach the boy concentration even under the toughest conditions. After a golf date, father and son would discuss every aspect of the day's play, usually with Earl picking apart Tiger's technique and suggesting possible improvements for the next practice session. Sometimes, the boy would get mad, but mostly he just got tougher, until, by age 8, Tiger had a focus and a coolness that could rival any adult's.

High-Profile, High-Pressure

Between ages 8 and 15, Tiger won the Optimist International Junior World championship six times, and became the youngest player ever to win the "Big I" – the Insurance Youth Golf Classic National. He was hot stuff and getting hotter (at age 15, he won 8 major junior championships, and was voted "Player of the Year" by several sports organizations). The game was still fun for him, and he loved competing, but superstardom carries a high price for any wunderkind. High exposure and intense attention often lead to burnout, bitterness and mental fatigue. Popularity did, indeed, add pressure to Tiger's life, and now and then he showed its signs, but what's remarkable is that he survived those years to become the composed young man he is today.

Reflecting now on his early celebrity status, Tiger credits the help and advice he got from Arnold Palmer, Jack Nicklaus and basketball star Michael Jordan with helping him keep his head. Jordan, Tiger says, sympathized: "What Michael told me is that I had it so much harder than he ever had it because he had five or six years before [big-time fame] happened to him. . . . He had time to adjust and build into it." Tiger recalls that Jordan's best piece of advice was when he told Tiger, "You're gonna make mistakes. The key is to learn from them as fast as possible."

Stanford University, one of the most prestigious universities on the West Coast, was home to Tiger Woods for two years before he turned pro in 1996.

Tiger Tries To Blend In

When he entered Stanford University as a freshman in 1994, Tiger was 18 and he was bringing with him an incredible 4.3 high school grade-point average. He was about to move from fairway superstar to studious economics major, and reportedly looked forward to being just another normal kid. But even at the top-rated school, where every student was a standout of some sort – a mathematics genius, a rocket scientist, a political mover and shaker – Tiger couldn't quite be thought of as average.

For one thing, he was fresh from an astonishing victory at the 1994 U.S. Amateur Championship – in fact, he'd missed Stanford's freshman orientation to attend the tournament – and his face was still being broadcast to every television set in America. For another, he was getting congratulatory phone calls from the likes of Jesse Jackson and invitations to appear on television talk shows with hosts Jay Leno and David Letterman. Still, Tiger viewed himself as nothing special among his peers. "If it's not the nation's best pianist, or the nation's best swimmer, it's somebody with a brain you

Jack Nicklaus presents Tiger with the Jack Nicklaus College Player of the Year award on June 2, 1996.

AP/WWP

can't believe," he said. "I'm just lost in a crowd here [at Stanford], which is fine. That's why I came."

Tiger's first contact with Stanford had actually come years earlier, when he'd been just 13 and was featured in *Sports Illustrated*. The Stanford golf coach, Wally Goodwin, after seeing the article on Tiger, was so impressed that he wrote the boy a letter inviting him to apply to the school when it was time for him to go to college. Tiger was excited at the prospect of attending a big-name school (he probably didn't even realize what an asset he'd be to the institution!), and wrote back to Coach Goodwin, thanking him for the honor of his recognition. In that letter, Tiger discussed his future plans to obtain a degree and become a PGA golfer. Even that young, Tiger was busy planning his life, weighing his options, looking ahead in a way that some adults never even manage.

A Buffer Against The World

That same Coach Goodwin proved to be a sanity-saving ally when Tiger did enter Stanford. Tiger's career – and, therefore, his media value – were skyrocketing, and people everywhere were clamoring for interviews, introductions and information. Had the coach not protected the young man's privacy – he made all callers, even team members, go through him before reaching Tiger by phone – things could have become very unruly, very fast.

As it was, the combination of studying, attending classes, playing on the Stanford golf team and entering national tournaments made for an incredibly busy life. Tiger says that he was able to keep up with his schoolwork by applying some of the skills he'd learned as an athlete. "Golf," he says, "taught me how to concentrate, how to focus for long periods of time. I was able to take that

The Letter Of A Lifetime

Coach Goodwin kept the original letter Tiger wrote him at age 13. In that initial correspondence, Tiger told Goodwin:

"I am working on an exercise program to increase my strength. By April, my NCGA handicap is one and I plan to play in SCGA and maybe some AJGA tournaments this summer. My goal is to win the Junior World in July for the fourth time and to become the first player to win each age bracket. Ultimately I would like to be a PGA professional. Next February, I plan to go to Thailand and play in the Thai Open as an Amateur."

Even then, Tiger was eloquent and determined to map his expansive future.

lesson into the classroom. I was able to close everything else out to study and complete the task at hand."

Tiger was also able to apply the discipline his mother had enforced throughout his earlier schooling. At home, the rule had been "no golf before homework," and that same set of priorities served Tiger well in college. Reflecting on Tiger's Stanford years, Coach Goodwin has remarked, "In my many years of coaching, he is the most focused in terms of the important aspects of his life and his goals. He is a giver, not a getter, and a product of two amazing parents."

Turning Pro

AP/WWP

Tiger offers his famous fist pump after sinking a birdie on the 16th hole of the U.S. Open in 1999.

The question on everyone's minds while Tiger was at Stanford was, "Will he or won't he turn pro?" During his freshman and sophomore years, he played – and won – numerous college and amateur tournaments, and people speculated that the lure of big professional bucks couldn't be denied for long. The young star and his parents maintained that Tiger would finish his education, that money was not an issue. Tida, said, "I don't want my son to be some kind of dumb athlete. I tell him, 'It's more than a piece of paper. That education in your head, no one can take it away.'"

In fact, neither money nor academics were the issues that finally pushed Tiger into leaving Stanford to pursue a professional career. The major factor was, as Earl Woods put it, the NCAA's "nickel-and-diming." College athletes are not, of course, allowed to make money at their sport, and a long and discouraging series of investigations was aimed at Tiger to make sure that he had not broken this rule. On one occasion, after playing in the Masters and publishing an event diary in *Golf World* and *Golfweek*, Tiger was suspended from college play for one day.

Problems like these occurred over and over again – once he was accused of accepting free equipment when he borrowed a golf club from a pro golfer – and eventually these stresses, combined with his academic workload, conspired to make Tiger as tired and listless as he'd ever been in his career.

Andrew Redington/AllSport

No situation is too tough for Tiger to tame. Here, he finagles out of the rough in the 1996 British Open.

To his father, he seemed bored by collegiate competition, and to the world at large, he seemed exhausted. In 1996, during his sophomore year, Tiger won a whopping 10 tournaments (including his third U.S. Amateurs), played at the British Open, and silenced the rumor mill by announcing his jump to professional status – at the same news conference where he revealed he'd signed a $60 million contract with Nike. He'd promised his parents, he said, that one day he would finish his degree, but for now Tiger would be concentrating only on golf.

Making The Most Of His Name

Tiger had been in demand before turning pro, but that was nothing compared to the hysteria which followed his move to the PGA. Crowds gathered at every venue he played to get even the slightest glimpse of him. The 20-year-old golfer was a genuine cult figure, with young female fans screaming, "I love you!" whenever he passed. It was unnerving, but at the same time, Tiger said that he was happy to see the galleries filled with young people.

This large black and white mural appeared on the side of a building in downtown Portland, Oregon.

Perhaps it was those crowds of youth, or perhaps it was the memory of his own early love of the green, but at any rate, something that year set Tiger's mind on giving something back to the world – specifically to the world of young, would-be golfers. With a personal donation of a half-million dollars, he established the Tiger Woods Foundation, whose aim was to support organizations which, from the platform of golf, "encourage youth to dream big dreams." Among the Foundation's goals are to "acquaint youngsters with the power they possess to improve their own circumstances," and to "encourage youngsters to care about and share with others." Tiger's name attracted millions of additional dollars in corporate donations, and a dream was born, one based on lessons his father had repeated throughout his son's life: You gotta care, and you gotta share.

In addition to infusions of cash, Tiger offers a good deal of his personal time to Foundation events. At golf clinics, Tiger provides one-on-one advice to kids about their stances, swings, and techniques – "This is how your grip should look" – and often delivers moving motivational speeches, as well. Earl, too, works hard to encourage the program participants, telling

Record Setter

In 1996, Tiger became the only golfer to ever win the U.S. Amateur Championship three years in a row.

them, "Don't set a limitation on your dreams. They can come true." And in a moving letter on the Foundation's website, Tiger writes about the valuable lessons that he's learned while playing golf, and now hopes to pass them on: "Do your best. Play fairly. Embrace every activity with integrity, honesty, and discipline. And above all, have fun."

And fun these kids surely do have. Among the past events sponsored by the Foundation have been pro golf exhibitions, celebrity auctions, clinics, camps, and activities of all sorts. State and local agencies often get involved, proposing a youth-oriented event and contacting the Foundation for support. Thousands of underprivileged kids have benefitted from these efforts. As Tiger says himself, he's a role model who takes his responsibilities seriously.

AP/WWP

Tiger's always willing to give a young golfer a private lesson during one of his junior golf clinics.

Sergio Garcia congratulates Tiger after his win at the Bay Hill Invitational in 2001.

AP/WWP

Lending A Helping Hand

Tiger has become a mentor to other golfers as well as to his fans. Sure, he is still learning to deal with his fame – but he's also passing along what he has learned so far to other young golfers. In 1999, during an informal round of golf, he offered advice and guidance to up-and-comer Sergio Garcia of Spain. As Tiger put it, "He's being besieged by people and for a person as young as he is, that's not easy to deal with." In hopes of helping someone else the way he himself was helped, Tiger shared some of his experiences with Garcia, pointing out both the good and the bad ways he'd handled them.

Race And Social Issues

Another thing Tiger that began to take more seriously after turning pro was his rare status as a successful minority golfer. As an amateur, he'd been concerned with becoming the best player of any kind, but upon signing with Nike, he appeared in a number of heavy-hitting commercials emphasizing

> "He will win more majors than Arnold Palmer and me combined."
> – Golf great Jack Nicklaus on Tiger's future in golf

the racial inequities which still exist in the world of golf. In one highly-publicized segment, Tiger said into the camera, "There are still courses in the U.S. I am not allowed to play because of the color of my skin." Many people criticized the ad because Tiger himself could, of course, play anywhere he liked. Others pointed out the basic truth of the message – that however Tiger's own status had changed, the average non-white golfer was still restricted from a number of prestigious golf clubs.

In his travels, Tiger learned from the older generation of black players – Jim Thorpe, Charlie Sifford, and

Lee Elder displays his trophy after winning the Monsanto Open Golf tournament in 1974.

others – what it had been like to play while competitors and observers muttered racial slurs. He then gained a whole new appreciation for those who had laid the groundwork for his own, relatively obstacle-free, career.

Honor And Tradition

In a tender, off-camera moment after becoming the first African-American to win the Masters Tournament, Tiger walked up to Lee Elders – who'd been the first African-American to play in the Masters at all – hugged him, and murmured, "Thanks for making this possible."

AP/WWP

Earl is always waiting to congratulate his son, no matter how Tiger fares on the course.

Keeping It In Perspective

On several occasions, Tiger has said that there are more important things in life than golf. (Homework, for one!) The depth of this belief has been apparent more than once, when the master of focused concentration lost his game because these higher priorities intervened. At a 1996 tournament in which Tiger should have been at his best, he shocked players and onlookers alike by driving one bogey after another throughout the day. His bearing was composed, if a little withdrawn, and everyone wondered what on earth was going on. He lost the tournament, and it wasn't until he was cutting short his time with reporters that the truth came out: He'd been up all night with Earl, who'd gone to the hospital with chest pains. "I love my dad to death," Tiger told them all. "And I'm going to see him right now." Reflecting on that day's round, Tiger's playing partner, John Cook, said, "He showed me a lot today, and it wasn't golf. . . . To hold his demeanor like he did was more impressive to me than some of the drives he tried to hit."

Earl's illness turned out to be a combination of pneumonia and some blockage in the coronary arteries. He was released from the hospital after a few days, but by the next year was hospitalized again, this time for triple bypass surgery. That day, too, Tiger was scheduled for a tournament, and played with less than his usual brilliance. Four days later, when surgical complications led to a second operation for Earl, the tension caused Tiger to be short and snappish with reporters. He played a televised tournament in which he tied for 20th place. And although Tiger never likes to lose, he remarked afterward, "I'm happy with what I did considering everything that is going on. It was hard to get a real deep focus because I was thinking about more important things than a round of golf."

Friends and family gathered to help Tiger celebrate his 22nd birthday at the All Star Cafe in Las Vegas on December 30, 1997.

Only later would it come out that Earl's second operation had been very serious indeed, a situation which would have caused many people to withdraw entirely from their responsibilities. But not Tiger. He knows his responsibilities as a athlete and always lives up to them. He is a true professional.

Allsport

Tiger shows off his 2001 ESPY Award for "Male Athlete Of The Year."

In A Word

If you were pressed to find a single word synonymous with Tiger Woods, the possibilities would be endless. "Integrity" would certainly make the list, given that this young man was raised to believe in the tenets and values that he still continues to live by. "Focus" would be another option, because if Tiger has learned anything from his early at-home golf training, it was how to fully concentrate on the task in front of you. But no, probably the best word for Tiger Woods would be "joy," for as Tiger himself has said in the past, "The great thing is that I get to do something I've always dreamt of doing, ever since I was a little kid watching Nicklaus on TV or watching Watson play well or all those great players play. I'm out here now with them, playing."

And by using the past as a yardstick to measure success, we now know that Tiger's not just playing – he's playing to win.

Hanging Out With Tiger

Tiger Woods has reinvented the game of golf and seems to have everything in the world that he could ever want – athletic ability, fame and wealth. His work ethic and raw talent have made him the most famous golfer in the world. Sometimes it seems that Tiger must have a single-minded focus on golf. But there is more to Tiger than meets the eye.

As a very young child, Tiger's father Earl hit golf balls with him, and as the years (and tournaments) went on, it became clear that Tiger was a golf prodigy. This combination of commitment and talent has made him a golf legend. After only four full years as a pro, he has won over $20 million in prizes and has made much more than that in his endorsement deals with the likes of Nike and Buick.

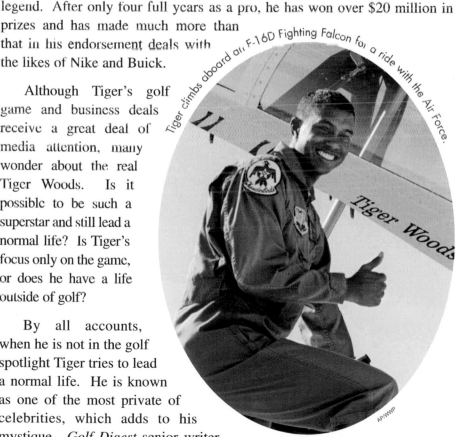

Tiger climbs aboard an F-16D Fighting Falcon for a ride with the Air Force.

Tiger Woods

AP/WWP

Although Tiger's golf game and business deals receive a great deal of media attention, many wonder about the real Tiger Woods. Is it possible to be such a superstar and still lead a normal life? Is Tiger's focus only on the game, or does he have a life outside of golf?

By all accounts, when he is not in the golf spotlight Tiger tries to lead a normal life. He is known as one of the most private of celebrities, which adds to his mystique. *Golf Digest* senior writer

Pete McDaniel has said, "I don't see him out having dinner like other players. He stays in his room during tournaments and I guess does room service. He can't go many places without being mobbed like a rock star." In interviews, Tiger will smile pleasantly when asked a question he does not want to answer and say politely, "Some things just have to be private." He does enjoy some of the benefits that come with his large paycheck, however. Once such perk is a private jet, which he uses to fly to tournaments, sometimes bringing friends and fellow golfers along with him. He also took flight with the Thunderbirds in Las Vegas, hitting zero gravity in an F-16 airplane.

A Loyal Friend

So who does Tiger hang out with, anyway? "I don't think he works hard to be one of the guys," says his golf buddy, Stewart Cink. "He has people his age, like me, who he's known for a long time." Some of his close friends are other sports luminaries like L.A. Lakers basketball player Kobe Bryant, baseball star Ken Griffey Jr. (whom he has taken batting practice with) and Michael Jordan, who helped Tiger deal with his sudden fame.

Tiger takes in a Chicago Bulls game in 1997.
Michael Jordan has become a mentor to Tiger over the years.

He is also very close with Mark O'Meara, his golf mentor, and has a group of loyal friends from high school and college. One of his other buddies is fellow golfer David Duval, who briefly held the #1 player in the world position in 1999. The two have flown to tournaments together in Tiger's jet, and on one such trip – to Maui for the Mercedes Championships – they made a pit stop in Las Vegas for a quick lesson with Tiger's swing coach, Butch Harmon, and a few rounds at the blackjack table. According to Duval, "My stack [of chips] was smaller." Does Tiger dominate at everything?

If the golf thing doesn't work out, Tiger can always caddie for friend Jerry Chang, shown here at a 2001 tourney.

Jeff Gross/Allsport

Tiger is extremely loyal to those close to him. After he won the 2000 U.S. Open, he went to the Black Mountain Golf and Country Club in Nevada to join his buddy and former college roomie Jerry Chang, who was qualifying for the U.S. Amateur Public Links Championships. But Tiger wasn't making a celebrity appearance – he *caddied* for Chang! Imagine Tiger Woods, golf legend, carrying someone else's clubs! To friend and pro golfer Casey Martin, that's not a startling image. "That doesn't surprise me at all," said Martin in *PEOPLE* magazine. "Tiger wants to lead a normal life as best he can."

Tiger's quest to keep a low profile extends to his romantic relationships, as well. He and former girlfriend Joanna Jagoda dated for several years and spent much of their time together doing things like going to Lakers games and eating at local restaurants. Then a student at the University of California at Santa Barbara, Jagoda stayed behind the scenes while they were dating (although she could often be seen cheering him on at tournaments), not wishing to draw on Tiger's celebrity.

Did You Know . . .

■ That Tiger is said to watch ESPN's *Sportscenter* three times a day?

■ That, on a dare from a friend, he once ate 14 tacos in one sitting?

Enter The Critics

Of course, anyone in the public eye has their share of critics, and Tiger is no different. Since not much is known about his private life, Tiger's work ethic is often focused on, and has been criticized at times. His focus on golf

Kenneth "Babyface" Edmonds (right), receives an autographed flag from the Masters Tournament before performing in the inaugural "Tiger Jam I" benefit concert in 1998.

is so strong that he sometimes ignores the "obligations" of fame. For example, before the 2000 U.S. Open he opted not to go to a ceremony paying tribute to the late Payne Stewart, champion of the 1999 U.S. Open. Instead, he played a scheduled practice round. This bothered a few of his critics, but Tiger's response was, "I felt going [to the ceremony] would be more of a deterrent for me during the tournament, because I don't want to be thinking about it."

This kind of comment has caused some to believe that he is self-centered, spoiled and even egocentric. He's too angry, and has no fun on the course, they say. However, though Tiger is extremely competitive and demanding of himself, this

Tiger Jams!

As part of his Tiger Woods Foundation efforts, Tiger has sponsored four "Tiger Jams" concerts in California and Las Vegas to benefit the Foundation, as well as other charities. The concerts, which attract a star-studded audience, have featured such musical acts as Third Eye Blind and Christina Aguilera.

doesn't mean that he's insensitive or self absorbed. On the contrary, he realizes what he can do as a celebrity, and has set up the Tiger Woods Foundation for precisely that reason. The Foundation's goal is to help inner-city and disadvantaged youths get the support and tools they need to reach their dreams and goals. Tiger, through the Foundation, holds junior golf clinics across the country, giving kids one-on-one attention. Once, when asked his biggest goal, Tiger said, "My biggest goal, other than winning tournaments, is to make golf look like America. We're the melting pot of the world, all races and religions. I've grown through golf, and I want to have a positive impact on kids. I want every child in America to have the opportunity I had." He obviously doesn't just talk the talk – Tiger walks the walk.

Tiger is also very attentive to small children who want autographs or a word with their idol. He often attends Little League games in Florida to watch Mark O'Meara's son play ball. Says an Orlando neighbor, "kids are always asking him to sign things, and Tiger never turns down a request."

Tiger: A Typical Gen-Xer?

Though Tiger may shun the media, he isn't entirely as serious as he appears. His friends say he has a great sense of humor.

And, in a lot of ways, Tiger is a typical "Gen-X" guy. "He'd rather hang out with his friends and play video games than anything else," says his swing coach, Butch Harmon, who once, while staying at Tiger's house, awoke in the middle of the night to find Tiger happily playing a new video game. Tiger has also been known as a fan of fast food, particularly McDonald's Value Meals (super-sized, of course). He often travels with a Game Boy while on the road, as well as a Ping-Pong table. According to *Golf Digest's* Pete McDaniel, Tiger enjoys playing his friends in "long, drawn-out matches. Tiger takes on all comers." Tiger used to travel with his own Sony Playstation console, but reportedly had to give that up to make more time for his training regimen. He even, according to a *Golf Digest* article, has a stereo system installed in his golf cart!

Most of all, it seems, Tiger just wants to be a regular guy. The evening before the 1997 Masters began, Tiger, who had rented a house near the course with some friends, relaxed by playing Ping-Pong and video games. He eventually wanted to shoot some hoops with his buddies. Unfortunately for him, Coach Harmon would have none of it. "I didn't want him to jam a finger," Harmon said. Ah, the travails of being Tiger.

Harry How/ALLSPORT

Proving that he's not serious all the time, Tiger and swing coach Butch Harmon laugh it up during a practice round at the 2000 British Open.

Tiger Tales

Fans love Tiger Woods for his cool steadiness, for his obvious passion for the game and for the zillion-watt smile he beams when things have gone his way. He seems like such a wholesome, all-American boy, with that baby face and that exuberant fist pumping the air at the successful end of a tournament. And it turns out that, behind the scenes, Tiger is just that – a big-hearted regular guy, albeit with a maturity beyond his years. Here, we've collected a few anecdotes that give some idea of the "real" Tiger Woods.

Waste Not, Want Not

Tiger and Mickey flash their famous grins for the camera after the 1999 Disney Classic.

He's a multimillionaire now, and could buy just about anything he wants, but Tiger doesn't seem to be a spendthrift. For example, it's been said that he wears a Mickey Mouse watch he got for free from Disney when he played in a tournament they once sponsored.

Sometimes Tiger's boyishness and middle-class background seem to betray him. Once, on the PGA tour, he looked at the courtesy car he was loaned to drive around, and said, "Wow! A Mercedes! I've never been in one!" Tiger's swing coach, Butch Harmon asked, "Well, why don't you go buy one?" Shocked, Tiger responded, "No way! Do you know how much this thing costs?" Then he took Butch out for a meal – at Taco Bell.

Feeling Bubbly

Everyone knows that Tiger has won the majors. The big question is – where does he keep those trophies? Tiger keeps them on his mantel, saying, "Originally, I was going to put them on my coffee table. But I have to confess: They look better up higher."

And they're not just for show, either – Tiger gets some use out of those trophies! Two of them served as celebration chalices. Tiger explains, "I have sipped champagne out of the U.S. and British Open trophies. You can't drink out of the PGA trophy because the top will fall off, and the Masters trophy is a replica of the clubhouse." Don't feel bad for him, though. Tiger says, "Just seeing them on the mantel brings a smile to my face."

It's All In His Head

Tiger says he doesn't really get frustrated when he hits a slump. "Obviously, I expect to win every time I play, but I know that isn't realistic," he has said. "The key is giving yourself chances. Golf is fickle and you can't force it. Sometimes the harder you try, the worse it gets."

According to Jay Brunza, Tiger's sports psychologist, Tiger "has the ability to raise his game when he has to. He's not going to burn out, because he plays for his own joy and passion."

Love Those Golden Arches

So what is the delicacy of choice for the world's greatest golfer? Ground beef on a bun, of course. It turns out that burgers are the food of champions – literally! Tiger, as the 1997 Masters champion, got to pick the menu for the next year's Champions Dinner. The golf great, of course, chose cheeseburgers and fries! And at one British Open, Tiger was thrilled to find two McDonald's and a Burger King between his hotel and the course; this meant he could have his favorite meal both to and from the practice rounds. "Just about wherever I go," he says,

Who Said Golf Isn't Dangerous?

About rising early to get in some tournament practice time, Tiger says, "I like to play early practice rounds because it is quiet and I can get more work done, not to avoid people . . . crowd control has been pretty good. I've gotten run over a couple times and my shirts still get marked up, but it hasn't been too bad."

"If there's a McDonald's there, I'll find it."

Unfortunately for Tiger, it seems that English fast food doesn't quite measure up to American fare. "The portions aren't as big," says the burger addict. "I order a super-size fries and get about as many as I get in a large in the States. The food isn't as greasy, either, and I really love the grease." Now that's a true fast-food connoisseur!

Tiger's fondness for burgers is well-known among his family and friends. After winning the 1996 Las Vegas Invitational, Tiger met with the press, shook many hands, heard many speeches, and then sat down to a big dinner with friends, colleagues and his mother. Famished from

During a 1997 practice session, Tiger takes a break to munch on his favorite food.

his successful day, he ordered a great big pepper steak from the menu and waited for it. Before long, waiters brought out hot plates with silvery covers, set Tiger's in front of him and whisked away the lid to reveal – two hot

A Very Important Call

President George W. Bush phoned Tiger to congratulate him after winning the 2001 Masters. His words to the new champion: "You make me proud to be an American."

The Tao Of Tiger

Tiger attributes his remarkable calm on the links to his Buddhist mother's influence. "[Buddhism] has given me the inner peace and calmness I probably would not have achieved at such an early age," he says. So does he actively practice Buddhism? Not exactly. "I practice it now and then when I feel like it," Tiger says.

McDonald's cheeseburgers. The little joke went over in a big way, and Tiger relished every bit as he dug in.

He's Got Some Nerve

Tiger is one of those rare people who actually thrives under pressure – maybe because his dad piled it on during every one of his childhood golf lessons! But that's not to say this superstar doesn't get nervous. "Nervous is good," he says. "It means you care. I want to play the person who isn't nervous, because I know I can beat him." He says the key is to know how to manage your anxiety, and that golf "is a great game because it teaches you to control your emotions and I'm a better person because of it."

Tiger may have shocked his mom at the 1994 U.S. Amateur Championship, but he still won.

APWWP

But not everyone in Tiger's world welcomes the stress. During the 1994 U.S. Amateur Championship, the wonder boy's mom watched on TV as Tiger made an incredible wedge shot, driving the ball 139 yards and sending it to rest just three feet from the edge of the water. "That boy almost gave me a heart attack," Kultida would later tell reporters. "All I kept saying was, 'God, don't let that ball go into the water.' That boy tried to kill me."

Scary Incident

One night, while a student at Stanford, Tiger was mugged on the way back to his dorm after a San Francisco charity dinner. A man jumped him in the parking lot, threatened him with a knife, and, when it turned out Tiger wasn't carrying his wallet, took his watch and a Buddha necklace. Then the man hit Tiger hard in the jaw with the butt-end of the knife before making a break for it.

Although it might have traumatized anyone else, Tiger handled the mugging the way he'd been taught at home – calmly and with concern for others. He walked to

Although he lost a valued Buddha necklace when he was mugged, Tiger still has another one. He carries it with him wherever he goes.

the student infirmary (though he wasn't badly injured), made a campus police report and called home. Hoping not to worry his parents too much, Tiger started the conversation on a light note: "Pops, you know that overbite I had? It's gone. My teeth are perfectly aligned." You gotta love him!

A Big Following

Few non-celebrities can understand what it means to be constantly sought out by reporters, TV personalities, tournament directors – just about everyone. Even mobs of adoring fans add to the feeling of being overcome by notoriety. One day, after watching Tiger being mobbed by people, a security guard outside a golf club locker room commented on Tiger's extreme fame. "I wouldn't give a nickel for it," was his response.

The
Legend

APWWP

The Bond Of A Lifetime

Was Tiger Woods born with a golf club in his hand? Just about, for according to his father, Earl Woods, "When Tiger was 6 months old, he would sit in our garage, watching me hit balls into a net . . . When he got out of the highchair, he had a golf swing."

Born on December 30, 1975, near Los Angeles in Cypress, California, to Earl and Kultida Woods, Tiger was often referred to by his father as "The Chosen One." There seemed to be a special bond between father and son right away. "When he was asleep, I would go to his crib and touch his cheek, and he would smile," Earl has said. "He knew it was me."

This bond paid off emotionally – and in the game of golf. By the time Tiger was 2 years old, he had enough training to putt against Bob Hope on the *Mike Douglas Show*. The following year, he shot a 48 for nine holes. His amazing ability put him on the pages of *Golf Magazine* when he was just 5. And through his youth, his drive continued, as he won the Optimist International Junior Tournament six times between the ages of 8 and 15.

The Woods Finishing School

How did these remarkable achievements happen? Did Tiger

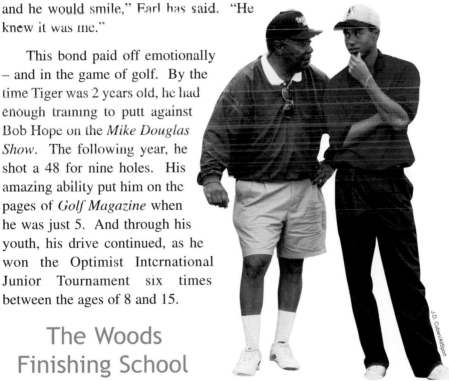

A pensive Tiger listens to his father's advice. Earl and Tiger have always had a special bond.

become such an incredible golfer simply by watching his father swing the club? Drawing from his experiences in the military as a Green Beret, Earl put Tiger through a rigorous six-month training session – which he called "The Woods Finishing School" – when Tiger turned 11. "Prisoner-of-war interrogation techniques, psychological intimidation – it went on and on," says Earl. "It was brutal." At the same time, Tiger's mother, Kultida (nicknamed "Tida"), was instilling in him the teachings of Buddha. This combination worked, as a few years later Tiger won the first of three consecutive U.S. Junior Amateur titles, followed by three straight U.S. Amateur championships. Butch Harmon, who was hired to help Tiger refine his swing in 1993, found himself "in awe of Tiger's raw power and natural ability . . . I thought, 'Look at that smile, look at that charisma. My gosh, he can really be something.'"

Just For The Fun Of It

And how did Tiger feel about the game and his accomplishments? He couldn't have enjoyed it more. "I absolutely loved it! I loved to practice. I loved to play. And more importantly, I loved to compete," Tiger replied when asked about his childhood. However, Earl was worried about Tiger obsessing over the game. He thought a 5-year-old should probably have more fun. But Tiger surprised his father by insisting that this "is how I have fun, shooting low scores."

Earl did try to make sure that the game stayed fun – and made sure that it was something they could do together, as father and son. "We had this

AP/WWP

In His Own Words

"I love this game to death. It's like a drug I have to have. I take time off sometimes because of the mental strain it puts on you. But when I'm competing, the will to win overcomes the physical and mental breakdowns."
– Tiger Woods

contest. I said, 'Let's see how many three-foot putts you can make.' When he got to 70 and I hadn't putted yet, I said, 'Tiger, this is ridiculous!' And he said, 'Daddy, this is fun!'"

More Than A Game

Though golf was fun, Earl wanted to use the sport to teach Tiger other lessons, as well. "I was using golf to teach him about life, about how to handle responsibility and pressure," explains Earl. Coach Rudy Duran backs Earl up, saying: "With Earl, there was no sulking or pouting when he didn't play well. Tiger learned by watching Earl in action."

And Tiger took his father's instructions to heart and was rarely disobedient, on or off the course. "He's never been chewed out or spanked," says his father. "He never even had a babysitter his entire life. You wanted to be around Tiger." Though some have suggested that Earl may have pressured his son into the game, even forced him to play at times, others who know the family well say that he never pressured Tiger. "Tiger was not a Jennifer Capriati [the tennis star whose pressured childhood has been well chronicled]," says Duran. "Earl wasn't pushy at all. He let Tiger do what he wanted with golf."

A young Tiger concentrates on his shot during the Los Angeles Open which was held at the Riviera Country Club in 1992.

It seems that Earl's teaching techniques have not hurt Tiger in any way. "A couple of times, Tiger has brought up the military experience that his father had, the toughness, the fighter in him," says golf pro Mark O'Meara, Tiger's close friend who lives near him in Orlando, Florida. "Tiger feels like he's inherited some of that."

Tiger digs out of the sand in Tulsa. Distracted by his father's failing health, Tiger shot an 8-over-par 78 that day.

Tiger, known for his cool, calm demeanor on the course, did occasionally get nervous. In 1992, when he played his first PGA tour event at the Riviera Country Club in L.A., the 16-year-old was standing near the opening hole when a "rigor mortis set in and his hands could barely grip the club." Even though he was as nervous as any other teen would have been on the links that day, Tiger was there for a reason. Most kids would use a driver on the par-5 opening hole, but Tiger selected a 3-wood, because he understood the game as an adult would. This knowledge put Tiger ahead of other young players.

The College Kid Turns Pro

Tiger enrolled in Stanford University in 1994 and within two years, he had won 10 collegiate events, among them the NCAA title. He also won the 1994 Western Amateur tournament. In 1995, Tiger participated in his first major championships (as an amateur), and made the 36-hole cuts in the Masters and the British Open. He unfortunately could not participate in the U.S. Open that year because of an injured wrist. In 1996, he made the cuts in two out of three championships he participated in. Tiger dropped out of Stanford to turn pro after his sophomore year and won two of his first seven tournaments, placing among the top 30 money winners and qualifying him for the Tour Championship. He was the first rookie since 1990 to win two tournaments, and was the first player since 1982 to have five top-five finishes in a row.

Passing The Torch

Earl is still highly involved in Tiger's life – he sits as president of Tiger's corporation ETW, and helps oversee his endorsements. Earl also helps keep Tiger focused and centered. However, Earl has had to step back from his involvement in his son's career as a result of his heart attack in 1996. When it happened, Earl was taken to a hospital near his Tulsa, Oklahoma, hotel, where he was staying while Tiger played in the Tour Championship. Tiger rushed to be with his dad at 2 a.m, even though he had to play a round the next morning.

The following year, Earl underwent triple-bypass surgery. Again, Tiger was there, right by his side. Earl has since paid increasing attention to his health. He also believes that the heart attack "deepened our sense of vulnerability, that it could end. It has forced Tiger to prepare for that eventuality."

With failing health, Earl has let go of Tiger, traveling to tournaments less frequently and handing off many of the day-to-day decision-making for ETW. He now keeps an eye on Tiger from a distance. As Tiger becomes more autonomous, more independent, the bond still exists. "There is a geographical separation," says Earl, "but there's no separation of the heart." Some bonds just can't be broken.

Lucy Nicholson/Image Direct

Tiger and his father, Earl, take a moment to pose for the cameras at an April 2000 Tiger Woods Foundation golf clinic.

The Zen Of Tiger

A great golfer needs a combination of intense focus and inner strength to succeed on the the links. So how does Tiger do it all? Two words: mental discipline.

Much has been said about Tiger Woods' athletic gift. He's been called a prodigy, a genius, even an athletic god. However, Tiger's great performance is a result of his hard work and lots of time spent on the course. His disciplined routine, technique, and training regimen make his performances almost flawless. This, combined with Tiger's inner philosophy – he was taught Buddhism by his mother at a young age – makes Tiger an unstoppable figure. Tiger's habits, preparations and philosophies make his game one of the greatest in the history of golf. But the presence of Tiger's mind has more to do with it than the strength in his swing.

AP/WWP

The Middle Eastern heat isn't enough to break Tiger's concentration as he practices for the 2001 Dubai Desert Classic.

Tiger's Tournament Prep

Tiger's behavior is quirky, to say the least, when preparing for a tournament. He demands order and routine at all times. Some say he's even a bit obsessive. Demanding absolute perfection on the course, Tiger will sometimes pick lint off the greens. He has many personal eccentricities, such as applying eyedrops or loudly blowing his nose. However, right before hitting the ball, Tiger's entire demeanor will change. "All players have some pre-shot routine," says Nick Faldo, whose British Open record was broken by Tiger at St. Andrews in 2000. "Tiger has blitzed all that. There's no twitch, no lift of the hat, no wasted energy."

So what does Tiger do to ensure that he'll perform his best during a tournament? Believe it or not, his rituals are very simple. He believes in a good night's sleep, sleeping well but "fast," as Tiger says. When he gets up, he's focused. And he knows he'll need to keep his focus for long periods of time. In Tiger's words, "you need to have [focus] for maybe two hours and then shut it off, come back home, rest up, do your whole routine all over again. And when you come back out, know that you've got a long day ahead of you."

No pre-game ritual is as helpful to Tiger as the mental concentration he learned from his mother.

AP/WWP

Tiger's Spiritual Game

There's something very spiritual about Tiger's preparation for the game. His Buddhist mother calls him the "Universal Child," while his father, Earl Woods, has called his son the "Chosen One," and even compared him to Gandhi. Although these comparisons seem a bit extreme, Tiger has become one of the most dominant athletes in the entire history of sports. Other athletes have begun to look at him in mystical terms, too.

Practice Makes Perfect

During some of his practice sessions, Tiger has been known to make himself sink 100 six-foot putts in a row. Try doing *that* sometime!

"He is something supernatural," says Tom Watson, who's been hitting the links since before Tiger was even born. Though Tiger may have doting, proud parents, does Tiger's spiritual philosophy have something to do with his incredible scores?

Tiger concentrates on a tricky putt on the 14th green during the 2000 Players Championship.

AP/WWP

Whether spiritual or otherwise, Tiger believes in bringing a balance to the game. When asked how he maintains a rhythm when swinging hard, he says, "I was always taught to maintain my balance throughout my golf swing, the entire ball flight and until the ball finished rolling, without having to struggle to achieve balance."

This talk of achieving balance is very "zen-like," very spiritual. Golf is often called a mental game, and Tiger's understanding of this goes deeper than most. To be a great golfer, it is important to stay in the moment, and free yourself of worry or anxiety. You can't be upset about a mistake you made earlier, or worry about making it again. And you can't really think about winning, either.

The face of a champion – Tiger waits to tee off during the second round of the 2001 Masters at Augusta.

APMWP

Tiger's game requires lots of practice, but when he tees off during a tournament, victory is never his main concern. In fact, he always maintains his focus in an attempt to " . . . [t]ry to finish on a good note," he says. "If I can finish on a positive note, carry that same momentum into the afternoon, with the same positive vibes and the same concentration level, I think that's the most important thing. On a long day, it's very easy to get a little lackadaisical, let your mind drift a little bit, instead of staying in the present . . . and [getting] the job done . . . because you're tired and your legs are feeling a little sore. You just need to keep plugging along, and know that you have a long day ahead of you."

AP/WWP

Tiger points to his ball as it drops for a birdie on the first hole of a three-hole playoff against Bob May at the 2000 PGA Championship.

Tiger seems to agree with his father, who has said that time "is just a linear measurement of successive increments of now. Any place you go on that line is now, and that's how you have to live it." For Tiger,

A Study In Scarlet

Without fail, Tiger wears the color red in the final round of every tournament, since his mother feels that it's a lucky "power color" for him. It's a wonder professional golfers everywhere haven't redone their wardrobes in shades of maroon and magenta – yet.

that means never letting anything distract his attention away from the hole he's playing at the time. With a whole day of golf to contemplate, thinking about the 14th hole when you're putting on the 6th could wreck everything.

There Is No Why

It's interesting to wonder how Tiger acquired his attitude. Perhaps it has to do with his upbringing and the influence of his parents. As an interracial couple, Earl and Kultida Woods emphasized the importance of integration and fairness. Being part of the first mixed-race couple in their California town, Tiger experienced racism firsthand as a child, such as when older boys at his school called him "nigger" and pelted him with rocks. But, as Earl Woods said of such an experience in a *Sports Illustrated* article, "you don't turn it into hatred. You turn it into something positive. So many athletes who reach the top now had things happen to them as children that created hostility, and they bring that hostility with them. But that hostility uses up energy. If you can do it without the chip on the shoulder, it frees up all of that energy to create."

And Tiger has said his game has improved through the influence of his mother and her spirituality, as well. "I believe in Buddhism," Woods has said. "Not every aspect, but most of it. I don't believe that human beings can achieve ultimate enlightenment, because humans have flaws."

Perhaps this is why Tiger, "the person," almost seems to vanish before taking a shot. It's a very personal moment, a very internal experience. He also reveals little emotion in interviews after a match. He gives out very few personal details. He's calm, cool and collected. It's difficult for the public to get to know him; he

Tiger relaxes with a grin as he waits on the 5th tee of the Old Course at St. Andrews during a delay on the second day of the 2000 British Open.

rarely returns phone calls and only his close friends know what he's really like. However, Tiger's rituals, his philosophies, his understanding of golf and his fascinating performances all give his fans intriguing clues into who Tiger is as a person.

The Secrets Of Tiger's Success

There's more to Tiger Woods than an uncanny ability to play golf. He draws from his inner strength and years of practice to perfect his skills and keep him on top of his game.

Strategy

Tiger is known for making precise decisions on the golf course. He knows not to depend only on the club he selects, but how to use his physical strength, his concentration and his equipment together to move the ball to exactly where he wants it to go.

David Leeds/AllSport

Tiger lines up and visualizes his putt on California's Big Horn Golf Course.

When asked what his strategy is, he replied, "Hit a lot of fairways. And if I have the situations, fire at [the hole]; and if I don't, dump [the ball] on the green somewhere and move on." Obviously, Tiger was simplifying his methods. He's constantly strategizing, carefully choosing where to focus his swing, and where he needs to put the ball. Even when he's not on the fairway, Tiger can be found strategizing about where to hit the ball and how to operate on the course. "When I'm [not swinging], I'm trying to pick sides of the fairway I want to hit the ball on," says Tiger.

With his unique combination of mind, body and spirit, Tiger has been giving his many competitors a run for their money!

Concentration

Mentally, Tiger is tough. He has the ability to drown out galleries populated by thousands of people, countless media cameras clicking inches from his face and the pressure of a competitor close on his heels. He also can chip his way out of a sand trap without flinching or seeming even slightly concerned.

"You can handle the rustling of feet. You can handle people yelling on other parts of the golf course . . . but a camera, it's foreign to golf."

— Tiger on noise

When he was training at an early age, Tiger's father would create diversions to force his son to concentrate through any distraction or problem. Then he would go home, where his mother guided him in meditation and taught him discipline.

Tiger has said that he's most comfortable when he's on the golf course and that the greatest lesson he ever learned there was how to be patient. And though he's honed his concentration skills all his life, he still has to make clear attempts at staying focused: "[Golf] takes a lot of concentration, and with all the distractions that can happen, it takes one who is very focused and very disciplined and knows what he wants."

Whether he's in between shots or lining up the perfect swing, Tiger is always focused on his game.

J.D. Cuban/AllSport

Strength

"Physical fitness is another part of my commitment to improve," says Tiger. "Soon after joining the tour, I realized that I needed to be stronger to handle its demands and build a consistent swing. So I worked hard to put on 20 pounds of muscle. I maintain my conditioning through a daily variety of cardiovascular exercises and weight training."

Rumors run rampant about Tiger's ability to bench press over 300 pounds, but Tiger refuses to discuss the specifics of his daily workout regimen. While some golfers don't think their game can be improved with a

AP/WWP

little more muscle tone, Tiger is very willing to explain his theory on shaping up. "It's difficult to compete against players who are so much stronger than you," Tiger explains. "In any other sport, if you're not stronger, you're either going to get your butt kicked, run over, [or] someone is going to hit more home runs than you. You just need to be stronger to keep up." Fans and professionals agree that Tiger's overall game has improved as a result of his dedication to fitness. And his winning golf scores are yet another testament to that.

Along with increasing muscle mass, Tiger has worked to stay flexible. Here, he stretches waiting to tee off.

Practice

What would you do if you were a professional golfer who just won the four biggest tournaments in the span of one year? Would you call it quits on practicing? Take a few months off in Aruba and spend your days sipping Mai Tais? Not Tiger. He's out on the course every day perfecting his game.

A Full Day

Tiger's normal regimen of practicing his swing involves hitting up to 1,000 balls in a single day!

"Perfection is always elusive in golf," says Tiger. "But that doesn't mean you can't strive to be the best you can be. To improve, you have to pay your dues on the practice tee and around the green. That means putting in extra time and effort to develop your skills. Nothing is ever given to you. You have to earn it."

The practice tee is where Tiger can get creative with his skills; he can work on getting out of any foreseeable situation. "He is still getting better and that shows great determination," observes golf legend Byron Nelson. "A lot of young people would not work to play better. They'd be satisfied. But he's the best player in the world, and he doesn't act like it. A lot of people don't want to work, don't have that inner drive. He wants to work. He really has a charge going."

Tiger knows that he's not going to sustain greatness by lounging on the green, which is why he's constantly out there, finding new ways to improve upon his game.

Jamie Squire/AllSport

Golf instructor Butch Harmon gives Tiger a few tips on chipping.

Swing

Tiger's swing is continually improving. Many golfers frequently discuss achieving that perfect swing, and once they find it, they rarely divert from it. Not Tiger. Woods is never convinced that the work on his swing is complete.

Phil Cole/AllSport

Tiger demonstrates his powerful swing to onlookers at his clinic in London.

"[Instructor] Butch Harmon and I basically built my golf swing as a team," says Tiger, and his mechanics are nearly flawless. Golf professionals have said that his swing is so effective because he's mastered the art of keeping his clubface square at the top of his backswing and through the entire motion. However, some of those same professionals also accuse Tiger of being over-eager during his downswing.

Tiger's professional game is still growing. He manages to put so much consistent power into his swing, yet he doesn't sacrifice accuracy for length, which is an amazing feat. According to Byron Nelson, "I don't think anyone has ever hit as consistently far as he does. I just don't see any weakness in his game."

"[Tiger] stood out like a sore thumb, because they were all swinging like babies, and he swung like he does now."

– TV talk show host Mike Douglas on Tiger's appearance on the show as a toddler

Tiger's Tools

Want to play like Tiger Woods? Now you have a chance. Here's the low down on the equipment that makes Tiger's growl just as big as his bite.

Golf has a new Superman in Tiger Woods, and everyone is rushing to the pro shop to stock up on all the equipment Tiger uses in hopes that some of the master's magic will rub off on their own game.

It's In The Bag

Golf regulations allow golfers to carry up to 14 clubs in their bag at once. Players can select any assortment of woods, irons, wedges and putters for their fairway arsenal as long as they do not exceed the standard count of 14 clubs. Tiger uses a titanium driver, a 3-wood and irons 2 through 9. He also packs three wedges, including a pitching wedge, sand wedge and lob wedge, and – of course – a putter.

The Driver: Technically, the driver is a 1-wood. It's the longest-hitting wood in the bag and it's used to literally drive the ball down the fairway. It can potentially send the ball sailing longer distances than any other club. But just because it's *called* a wood doesn't mean it's necessarily *made* of wood. Tiger's driver is a Titleist Titanium 975D.

Tiger uses the Titleist 975D as his driver.

Woods: Woods, the equipment that shares a name with Tiger, are used to achieve distances equal to or exceeding 200 yards, which is usually easiest to accomplish by getting the ball in the air. Tiger carries a 3-wood, a Titleist 13 degree.

Irons: Tiger carries irons 2 through 9. On average, using an iron can ensure that the golfer will send the ball from 120 yards (9-iron) to 190 yards (2-iron) down the fairway. The higher the iron number, the less distance the golfer can expect. Being able to judge the distance between the ball and the hole is key when selecting the most efficient iron for a particular shot.

Wedges: Wedges are handy for getting yourself out of the traditional golfing mishap. When you've landed in a bunker or the rough, or you need to fish your ball out of the pond, you need a tool that will get under the ball to achieve more dramatic lift and less distance than a wood. After all, you're not aiming too specifically when you're buried in sand, you're just trying to remove yourself from trouble. Just in case Tiger gets himself into a sticky situation on the course, he travels with a pitching wedge, a sand wedge and a lob wedge.

Putter: Putting is an art form. And Tiger doesn't get much of a choice in tools when he's on the course as he only travels with one putter at a time. Therefore, he has to know how to use his putter of choice in any given situation.

There are two main types of putters that players can choose from – heel-shafted and center-shafted. There's no big mystery here. On the heel-shafted putter, the blade meets the shaft at the back, very similar in design to a hockey stick. The shaft of the center-shafted putter meets the blade just

The swoosh lets everyone know that Tiger uses Nike's line of golf balls.

right of the middle and then bends approximately two inches up to achieve the same shaft angle as the heel-shafted putter. Tiger's putter of choice is center-shafted and is a Titleist Scotty Cameron prototype putter.

What's On The Tee

He's used both Titleist balls and Nike balls, but Tiger has finally settled on the Nike Precision Tour Accuracy TW, which has been molded to his personal specifications and his 125 mph swing. After all, the "TW" stands for Tiger Woods.

Club Cover

Peering out of Tiger's bag is a friendly, plush tiger head that protects his driver from the elements. Not all players use them, but Tiger's club cover is among his many signature accoutrements. But don't expect to find its feline sibling in any golf shop. This tiger is one of-a-kind, made specially for the golfer by his mom. And inside the cover is a special note, stitched in Thai, that translates into English as "Love from Mom."

Fitting Attire

Just slightly less important than the equipment you carry with you on the course is the "equipment" that you wear. From the olden days of wearing unforgiving tweed jackets to the polyester years and finally, up to today's cotton-comfort clothing phenomenon, wearing the proper golf attire requires almost as much strategy as trying not to bogey. First, your clothes must not hinder your swing but, a close second, to play like a champion you must look like one too!

Tiger is comfortable and stylish wearing Nike gear from head to toe.

AP/WWP

"When I was young, it wasn't cool to play golf. And there certainly wasn't anything cool to wear to play golf. I love it. It's all changing around," says Tiger. Which begs the question – would Tiger be just as suave in polyester?

If you look carefully at many of the photos of Tiger holding his various championship trophies, one thing stands out. He's wearing the same colors in all of them – red and black. On the last day of every tournament, Tiger dons a red shirt, or some similar hue, along with black pants.

And don't be surprised to see the golf prodigy adorned in Nike apparel. Tiger, who has a lucrative contract with the sportswear giant, created his own line of clothing for the company. In addition to Nike shirts, slacks and sweater vests, you can usually see him adorned in a Nike hat, which is easily recognizable by the company's trademark "swoosh."

It's The Shoes

With Tiger Woods' help, Nike developed the line of golf shoes Tiger wears on the links. And now everyone can purchase the Course Air TW spikes.

Shoes are a major part of the game. And to ensure he gets his best foot forward, Tiger developed the Course Air TW line of golf shoes with Nike. His preferences yielded a line of footwear that features the Q-LOK spike system, waterproof leather and, according to Nike, "the very best in designs, Italian fabrics and treatments."

Cross-Country And Back Again

Tiger isn't just a golfer, he's trained in other areas as well. "I tried other sports. I ran cross-country in high school. But golf was my sport," explains Tiger. And we're all very pleased that he traded in his sneakers for spikes.

Tiger Trivia

You may think that you know everything there is to know about Tiger Woods, but you may be surprised by some of the interesting bits of trivia we have unearthed about everyone's favorite golfer.

■ When Tiger was just 2 years old he played in a kids' tournament and won. And at the age of 3, he shot an amazing 48 at the nine-hole Navy Golf Course in his hometown of Cypress, California. In fact, he continued to play there much to the disappointment of his fellow golfers – he kept beating them!

■ If Tiger seems perfectly at ease in front of a television camera, it could be because TV appearances are nothing new to him. As a youngster, he was not only on *The Mike Douglas Show*, where he putted with Bob Hope, but also on *That's Incredible*.

■ When Tiger was a child, his primary hero (besides his father) was Jack Nicklaus. Tiger even hung a chart on his bedroom wall so he could compare his progress with that of his favorite golfer.

■ After winning his first professional tournament at the 1996 Las Vegas Invitational, Tiger's victory dinner was a unique one – two McDonald's cheeseburgers, washed down with champagne.

■ If you think Tiger got started golfing early, you won't believe how he first got involved with Stanford University. His photo appeared in *Sports Illustrated* after he won a junior tournament and it caught the eye of Stanford's golf coach, Wally Goodwin.

Goodwin sent a letter expressing his interest to the 13-year-old Tiger, who was not even in high school yet!

■ When a young Tiger hit his bag with his club after making a bad shot, his mom actually asked that her son be penalized two strokes for misconduct!

■ Playing golf requires a lot of mental discipline, and to help improve his game, Tiger worked with sports psychologist Jay Brunza. They even tried hypnosis to improve Tiger's score!

AP/WWP

Tiger's club has sported a special cover since the 1992 Nissan Open.

■ When Tiger was invited to play at the 1992 Nissan Open, he was still an amateur and became the youngest player ever to participate in a PGA tournament. At the event, he sported a special club cover made by his mom which looked like a tiger and said "Love From Mom" in Thai.

■ Tiger almost wasn't able to compete in the 1993 Junior Amateur Tournament as he had fallen ill with a bout of mononucleosis.

■ Tiger had an astounding amateur career. He was the youngest to win the U.S. Junior Amateur Championship – which he later won two more times – making him the first to win the U.S. Amateur Championship three consecutive times.

■ In 1999, Tiger had laser surgery to correct his vision. While it was probably to help his game, it may have been partially to rid himself of his hated college nickname, "Urkel." Reportedly, he did not enjoy being compared to the bespectacled geek from the TV show, *Family Matters*.

■ Tiger was the youngest Masters tournament champion in 1997, at the age of 21.

He's Pretty Humble

In an interview with *NBC News*, Tiger explained away his enviable position in life this way, "I am just like you guys. I'm a human being, and all I do is chase a little white ball around."

■ Tiger joined the ranks of Mary Lou Retton and Michael Jordan when he appeared on the famed Wheaties cereal box.

■ With his victory at the British Open in 2000, Tiger became the youngest player – at the age of 24 – to have won all four of the major championships.

■ In the 1862 British Open, "Old" Tom Morris triumphed and set the major championship record margin of 13 strokes – that is, until Tiger beat his score with a 15-stroke margin at the 2000 U.S. Open. Tiger also broke the U.S. Open record margin of 11 set by Willie Smith in 1899.

■ Also in 2000, Tiger was the second golfer to win three important majors in the same year. The only other golfer to do that was Ben Hogan in 1953.

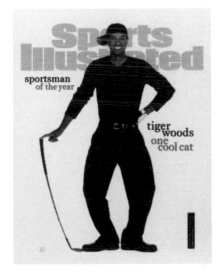

sportsman of the year

tiger woods
one cool cat

■ Ever since *Sports Illustrated* came up with their Sportsman of the Year award, only one athlete has ever received that honor twice. Tiger won it in 1996 and in 2000. He is only the sixth golfer to win the award since its inception in 1954.

■ Tiger has always claimed he grew up like all the other kids his age, " . . . addicted to T.V. wrestling, rap music, and *The Simpsons*."

■ In his professional career, Tiger has had two caddies working for him: Mike "Fluff" Cowan and Steve Williams.

■ While many other kids his age where listening to albums by their favorite cartoon characters; a 6 year old Tiger Woods was reportedly listening to motivational tapes.

A Record Of Excellence

Career Statistics

Tiger has taken on some of the world's toughest courses from Augusta to Pebble Beach and beyond. He's braved Midwestern mud, Pacific fog and even a crazed Scottish streaker to build his career into one worthy of the true professional he is.

When you're as new to the world of professional golf as Tiger Woods, no one expects you to do terribly well, right? Wrong. Since his professional debut at the age of 16, Tiger has gone from a junior amateur with potential to golf's #1 hero.

Year	# Of PGA Tournaments	Wins	Top 5	Top 10	Winnings	Standing
1992	1	0	0	0	N/A	Amateur
1993	3	0	0	0	N/A	Amateur
1994	3	0	0	0	N/A	Amateur
1995	4	0	0	0	N/A	Amateur
1996	11	2	5	5	$790,594	Turned Pro
1997	21	4	7	9	$2,066,833	Pro
1998	20	1	8	13	$1,841,117	Pro
1999	14	7	8	12	$6,616,585	Pro
2000	20	9	15	15	$8,286,821	Pro
2001*	8	3	6	7	$3,263,857	Pro

* as of the 2001 Masters

PGA Victories

Dates	Tournament	Par	Rounds					Total Score	
			1	2	3	4	5		
Oct. 2-6, 1996	Las Vegas Invitational	72	70	63	68	67	64	332	-27
Oct. 17-20, 1996	Walt Disney Classic	72	69	63	69	66		267	-21
Jan. 9-12, 1997	Mercedes Championships	72	70	67	65	r/o		202	-14
April 10-13, 1997	Masters Tournament	72	70	66	65	69		270	-18
May 15-18, 1997	Byron Nelson Classic	70	64	64	67	68		263	-17
July 3-6, 1997	Western Open	72	67	72	68	68		275	-13
May 7-10, 1998	BellSouth Classic	72	69	67	63	72		271	-17
June 3-6, 1999	The Memorial	72	68	66	70	69		273	-15
July 1-4, 1999	Western Open	72	68	66	68	71		273	-15
Aug. 12-15, 1999	PGA Championship	72	70	67	68	72		277	-11
Aug. 26-29, 1999	World Series Of Golf	70	66	71	62	71		270	-10
Oct. 21-24, 1999	National Car Rental Golf Classic	72	66	66	66	73		271	-17
Oct. 28-31, 1999	The Tour Championship	71	67	66	67	69		269	-15

Dates	Tournament	Par	Rounds					Total Score	
			1	2	3	4	5		
Nov. 4-7 1999	World Golf – American Express Championships	71	71	69	70	68		278	-6
Jan. 6-9, 2000	Mercedes Championships	73	71	66	71	68		276	-16
Jan. 31-Feb. 7, 2000	AT&T Pebble Beach National Pro-Am	72	68	73	68	64		273	-15
Mar. 16-19, 2000	Bay Hill Invitational	72	69	64	67	70		270	-18
May 22-29, 2000	Memorial Tournament	72	71	63	65	70		269	-19
June 15-18, 2000	U.S. Open	71	65	69	71	67		272	-12
July 20-23, 2000	British Open	72	67	66	67	69		269	-19
Aug. 17-20, 2000	PGA Championship	72	66	67	70	67		270	-18
Aug. 24-27, 2000	WGC-NEC Invitational	70	64	61	67	67		259	-21
Sept. 7-10, 2000	Bell Canadian Open	72	72	65	64	65		266	-22
Mar. 15-18, 2001	Bay Hill Invitational	72	71	67	66	69		273	-15
Mar. 22-26, 2001	The Players Championship	72	72	69	66	67		274	-14
April 5-8, 2001	The Masters	72	70	66	68	68		272	-16

Great Moments In Tiger's Career

Do you remember when Tiger Woods conquered his first Masters? Or when he played his first tournament as a PGA pro? Over the years, Tiger has given the world of golf some of its brightest moments and most memorable tournaments.

When Tiger Woods takes to the course, the gallery knows they're about to see a master at work. Throughout his career, Tiger's performances on the links have astounded every fan and broken just about every record in the book.

The 1992 Nissan Open

Sudden Death In Thailand

The PGA Tour isn't the only place where Tiger's skill shows through. At the 1998 Johnnie Walker Classic in Thailand, he ended up eight strokes behind Ernie Els and managed to score enough birdies by the 18th hole to tie with Els for first place. Tiger beat Els in the sudden death round.

At age 16, a time when most kids are still learning to drive, Tiger Woods' mind was busy with something else – playing as an amateur in the Nissan Open, his first PGA tournament. The young man knew he could hold his own at the Riviera Country Club in California, near his family's home in Cypress. As the youngest player ever to compete in a PGA Tour event, Tiger had to get special permission to be absent from school on the day of the tournament.

The truth is, Tiger wasn't so sure about his chances for success. "I might hit the ball farther than some of [the other players]," he said at the time, "but that doesn't mean anything. These guys have got their swings fine-tuned. I don't. They know exactly how far they hit it. . . . These guys are awesome."

Despite a sore back and the pressures of being a first-timer in a professional golf event, Tiger's performance was enough to impress even the most steadfast of golf veterans. In the first round, he shot 72, scoring a birdie and two bogeys before finishing with 75 in the second and missing the cut. Still, he managed to keep his spirits up throughout that first tournament experience.

The 1996 Greater Milwaukee Open

After almost two decades of honing his skills on the links and a few years of gracing the PGA tour as an amateur, Tiger was ready for his professional debut. Although he didn't accomplish an award-winning finish at the Greater Milwaukee Open, golf writers from coast to coast who saw Tiger's performance in Milwaukee raved about the youth's potential, touting him as one of the future greats.

Tiger finished the second round with a 69, and he expressed his happiness with his performance. "I was happy with a 69," he said. "That's two scores in the 60s, and you have to be pleased with that." Tiger completed the tournament at 277, 7 below par and tying for 60th place.

The 1996 Las Vegas Invitational

Barely two months into his rookie year, Tiger was ready for a professional tournament victory. And, in October of 1996, he finally tasted victory in the same city where so many people go to make their dreams come true – Las Vegas!

Upon arriving at the Las Vegas Invitational, Tiger was in for an extra round of competition, as the tournament goes for five rounds

AP/WWP

Tiger poses with his trophy and two of Bally's Jubilee dancers. He won the Las Vegas Invitational in 1996.

Tiger reacts after hitting a hole-in-one in the final round of 1996's Greater Milwaukee Open.

APWWP

instead of the usual four. The first round was not quite Tiger's best performance, leaving him with a score of 70 that Wednesday. But in the following round, three straight birdies and an amazing score of 63 – 9 under par for that course – were enough to put him back on top. By Saturday, Tiger had moved all the way from 83rd place up to seventh!

On the tournament's last day, it came down to Tiger and veteran golfer Davis Love III, who were both tied at 64. The sudden death playoff to settle the score was tense for Tiger and his caddie, Fluff Cowan.

On the first playoff hole, Tiger settled for a par. But Love's par putt sailed past the hole and Tiger clinched his first professional victory.

The pros at Las Vegas had been playing the links for years. Yet, on October 6, 1996, they were beaten by a young fellow who couldn't even legally drink his bottle of celebratory champagne.

The 1997 Masters Tournament

The greatest heroes of golf gather every April for The Masters Tournament, and fans worldwide know that they'll be seeing the best of the best compete at Augusta National Golf Club in Georgia, one of the finest courses in the United States. Yet, for over 60 years, every winner of that coveted Green Jacket had been Caucasian. In the spring of 1997, the record books would become outdated in many ways.

Despite a slow start on the first day, Tiger still managed to get away with fourth place. The following round's score of 66 – 6 under par for Augusta – sent him all the way to the top. But the third round was what really made golfers and fans take notice. Tiger played all 18 holes of the third round *without a single bogey.* That amazing score of 65 made it clear to everyone that the 61st Masters Tournament belonged to Tiger. "If he's playing well, the golf course becomes nothing," said Jack Nicklaus of golf's new star. "He reduced the golf course to nothing." When it was time for the all-important fourth round, Tiger left his competitors in the dust and was leading the tournament by an amazing nine strokes.

While focusing his mental energy on the 18th tee of the fourth round, Tiger was set to make par on the last hole and make Masters history when someone in the gallery took a picture. The sudden noise of the camera threw Tiger's concentration off, and he accidentally knocked the ball into the gallery! After he and his caddie, Fluff, frantically searched, they finally found the ball and Tiger was able to drive it straight to the 18th green, hitting the hole in two more strokes. By making par on the tournament's final hole, Tiger had not only won one of golf's highest honors, but set a record with a 270 for the tournament, a whopping 18 under par!

Nick Faldo helps Tiger into his new coat – the Green Jacket from the
1997 Masters Tournament.

But that wasn't all. His victory margin of 12 strokes set another Masters record. At the age of 21, Tiger was now the youngest golfer ever to win the Masters. And that wasn't his only accomplishment – Tiger was also the first golfer of African-American or Asian-American descent to win the all-important tournament.

As Tiger tried on that coveted Green Jacket, fans from every walk of life cheered. Not just for Tiger, but for every minority golfer who had ever been denied the opportunity to hit the links with everyone else.

The 1998 BellSouth Classic

Tiger completes his swing on the second hole of the final round in 1998's BellSouth Classic.

APWWP

Soon after conquering the Masters, Tiger encountered a long dry spell. Following a win at the 1997 Western Open, a 10-month string of losses began to follow him, leaving him winless on the PGA Tour until the spring of 1998.

That was the year when Woods showed the world that he wasn't done yet, finishing off the BellSouth Classic tournament in Duluth, Georgia, one stroke ahead of Jay Don Blake. Despite a shot that nearly landed in the water, Woods was happy to be back in the game. In fact, he was quick to answer critics when they wondered why he hadn't been successful lately. "I've been right there," was his answer. "I just haven't been able to get that one shot here or there to win it."

The 1999 PGA Championship

His winless streak a fading memory, Tiger was ready to take a stab at the PGA Championship in the summer of 1999. But he didn't count on two things: the elements and some very real talent to oppose him.

The golf course at Medinah, Illinois – known as the "Monster of the Midwest" – has never exactly been the easiest place in the world to play. And the inclement weather of August 1999 didn't make things easier for anyone, including Tiger. In fact, the torrential rain was so bad that play was suspended in the first round with 15 players left to go.

Additionally, Tiger didn't just blow past his competition with his usual ease. In fact, Tiger realized early on that winning this major wouldn't be a walk in the park. As 19-year-old Sergio Garcia took first place in the first round, Tiger was left stranded with a 2-under-par 70 in the first round. Then the second round saw longtime veteran Jay Haas sprinting ahead of Tiger, despite Tiger's five birdies in the first seven holes. Nonetheless, Tiger was happy with his improved score of 67. "I'm very pleased with the way I played under these conditions," he said. "Somehow, I was able to make par after par after par."

Tiger kisses the Wanamaker trophy after winning the 81st annual PGA Championship on August 15, 1999.

Tiger's amazing 50-foot birdie putt at the sixth hole was only one of his methods for shooting back up to the top in the third round. In the final round, Garcia was back in the running and seemed to be gaining. But Tiger's even par score of 72 put him a single stroke ahead of Garcia, and showed him that he still had a way to go before he could defeat a determined player like Tiger.

The 2000 U.S. Open

The 2000 tournament at the famed Pebble Beach golf course in California started out well for Tiger. He was on a roll as he played his way through a perfect bogey-free round, situating himself in first place with a 6-under-par 65 and setting a new record for the best score in a round at the U.S. Open. Then, a second round weather delay cut Tiger's tee time and only allowed him to finish 12 holes before twilight ended that day's play. Unfazed, Tiger prepared to resume his streak the following morning.

Tiger talks to the press during the 100th U.S. Open which was held in Pebble Beach, California in June of 2000.

On the morning of the second round, however, fans saw a whole new side of Tiger. When he teed up to drive the ball to the 18th hole, he mistakenly hooked his shot over Pebble Beach's infamous "Cliffs of Doom" and into the Pacific Ocean. Understandably frustrated, Tiger let loose a stream of audible obscenities that some found shocking. Despite his bogey on the last hole, Tiger recovered enough of his cool to finish up the second round with a 69.

Tiger's third round of the Open wasn't as impressive as he had hoped, since a triple-bogey at the third hole left him with a par-71 finish. But he was still leading the tournament by a hefty 10 strokes at the beginning of the last round. By the end of the Open, Tiger had won his third major championship and became the only player to finish the U.S. Open double-digits under par. A congratulatory phone call from President Bill Clinton made the occasion even more memorable.

But breaking records wasn't important to Tiger. "The only thing I know is I [have] the trophy sitting right next to me," he said after his victory. "To perform the way I did, and on one of the greatest venues in golf, it doesn't get much better than that."

Respect Your Elders

When Tiger won his first Masters, he was quick to credit Lee Elder, the first African-American golfer to play in the tournament. "It was because of people like [Elder] that I was able to turn pro, to get this opportunity," Tiger said at the time.

The 2000 British Open

Ever since suffering a triple-bogey in the third round of the U.S. Open, Tiger had been determined to avoid bogeys for as long as possible. For his first round at St. Andrews golf course, he was able to keep the streak going, as he played the first eight holes on par and finished five strokes under par. Even the topless woman who tried to rush the green when Tiger was working on the 18th hole during the last round couldn't break Tiger's determination to reign victorious at golf's oldest course. As usual, Tiger was more concerned with playing one hole at a time. "You can't let yourself look ahead to the final outcome," he said, "because if you don't take care of the present, the final outcome may not be what you think."

Tiger's "live for today" mindset paid off, even though the outcome was indeed what so many had expected. Tiger fans worldwide were overjoyed when their hero held aloft that silver trophy in Scotland. Not only had Tiger scored a golf career Grand Slam, he had succeeded in being the youngest player to ever do so. At the age of 25, a mere four years after turning pro, Tiger added his name to all four of golf's major championships – not only with victories, but with broken records all along the way.

Tiger's Trophies

There's the fame. There's the money. But what else do you get when you win a PGA Tour event? Tiger Woods' short career has earned him several trophies, many of which have stories that are as fascinating as the golfers who have won them beforeTiger was even born.

With its historical roots, golf is a sport with many traditions. And those traditions include the majestic ceremonies held after each tournament, when the victor is honored with a trophy.

However, those winners usually don't get to keep the fruits of their labor. Each trophy is up for grabs every year, and the previous year's winner has to return it so someone else has a chance to take it home. But all the winners' names go on those trophies, joining the ranks of amazing golfers who came before them.

AT&T Pebble Beach National Pro-Am

02/07/00

At Pebble Beach in California, players gather to compete next to the majestic Pacific Ocean. Where else can an aspiring golfer tackle such a challenging course, possibly end up with a Waterford Crystal trophy, then relax in the clubhouse with actor Clint Eastwood, who owns the course? Surely, that would make any golfer's day.

Harry How/AllSport

Bay Hill Invitational

03/19/00

In honor of golf's roots in Scotland, the Bay Hill Trophy is a stunningly crafted replica of a Wilkinson sword. So far, Tiger has yet to try using this unique prize to scare away his opponents!

British Open Championship

07/23/00

Honoring the days when upper-class English gentlemen wagered cases of wine on games of golf, the famous Claret Jug has been awarded to British Open winners for over a century. After the 1996 tournament, winner Tom Lehman gave it to a friend for safekeeping. Later that night, police picked up Lehman's friend and accused her of stealing it!

Las Vegas Invitational

10/06/96

Though he was just in his rookie year (in fact, this was only the fifth professional event that he entered), Tiger added this impressive trophy to his shelf when he won the Las Vegas Invitational in October of 1996. Today, the Las Vegas Invitational is known on the circuit as the Invensys Classic.

AP/WWP

David Cannon/AllSport

Masters Tournament

04/13/97

Pros worldwide dream of taking home the Masters trophy, a replica of the original silver miniature of the clubhouse at Augusta. But even more desirable is the stylish green jacket that goes with it – although, the winners don't get to keep that either. After a year, the jackets go back to Augusta where the winners can wear them at the banquet following the Masters.

PGA Championship

08/20/00

Professional golf owes a great deal to Rodman Wanamaker, the successful department store tycoon who founded the PGA in 1916. Without him, many believe that the PGA might not even exist. Therefore, in his honor, the PGA Championship named its coveted prize the "Wanamaker Trophy."

Donald Miralle

AP/WWP

Players Championship

03/26/01

At the official ceremony for the Players Championship, the winner just gets a replica of the trophy for photo opportunities. The winner then gets the real one sent to his home, with his name engraved on the front. But that's not all! The Waterford Crystal company also awards the winner with a 100-piece set of crystal. After all, you have to have something with which to toast your victory!

Golf Through
The Years

History Of Golf

A seemingly simple game of landing a ball in a hole has an extraordinary history. It has won over royalty, put nations in peril and helped America confront its racial tensions. With Tiger Woods at the helm, this sport is quickly becoming one of the hottest national pastimes.

Golf as we know it is believed to have originated in Scotland. Other games throughout history involving a stick and ball showed similarities to golf, however. During the days of the Roman Empire, the emperors played a game called "paganica" and used a bent stick to move a soft ball filled with feathers along. Over the next five centuries, various other versions of the game developed. In the 14th century, the Dutch played "kolven;" in the 16th century, the French developed "jeu de mail;" and the English played a similar game called "cambuca."

Bettmann/CORBIS

A lithograph depicts Scotsmen playing an early form of golf.

Evidence suggests that the French were also playing a game called "chole" as early as 1353. In 1421, the Scots went to France to help in a fight against the British army and might have been introduced to this precursor of golf at that time.

However, none of these earlier games involved one of the critical elements of golf – the hole. Rabbit runs – burrows dug by rabbits and sometimes enlarged by foxes – are thought to have provided the first "holes." This predecessor to modern golf is believed to have started in the 15th century on the eastern coast of Scotland. Players used sticks and clubs to knock a round object into the "hole."

The sport definitely caught on with the people of Scotland. Many of the early courses were built on the eastern coast where the wind and sea created hilly dunes. The game was free and accessible to everyone. Eventually, however, its popularity would be considered a threat to national security. In the 1400s, the Scots were at risk of an English invasion. The parliament of King James II worried that the kingdom's love of golf and soccer was caus-ing it to neglect archery practice. Both sports were banned in 1457 – the first documented reference to golf – and the sports were again banned in 1470 and

The eastern portion of Scotland, with its hilly dunes, created natural landscapes for early golf courses.

1491. Nonetheless, the Scottish people played on. The bans were lifted in 1502, under the reign of King James IV, who was an avid golfer. Once royalty caught on to the game, its popularity spread even further. And, by the 16th century, golf had spread to England and across the channel to France. The fears of Parliament, however, were ultimately shown to be justified. In 1513, at the Battle of Flodden Field, the Scots lost to the English. The archery skills of the English were no match for their golf-playing rivals.

Who Wouldn't Rather Be Golfing?

Aside from taking time away from archery practice, the game of golf caused other problems in Scottish communities, as well. Parishioners were often punished for playing golf when they should have been listening to sermons!

The first documented golf club was the Gentlemen Golfers of Leith in Scotland. It was founded in 1744 and its members drafted the first written rules for the game. One of the rules stated, "If a ball be stopp'd by any person, horse or dog, or anything else, the ball so stopp'd must be played where it lyes." Golf has come a long way since then — imagine a ball being stopped at the Masters by a wayward horse! The club later became the Honourable Company of Edinburgh Golfers in 1768. The Royal and Ancient Golf Club was established 10 years later in St. Andrews, and remains in existence today.

Golf became popular in America in the late 19th century.

Golf Comes To America

The Scotsman John Reid is considered the father of American golf. He formed the St. Andrew Golf Club in New York in 1888. Reid allegedly asked a fellow Scotsman to bring him some golf clubs and balls when he came back to the United States, and from those tools, the club was formed.

In 1894, the United States Golf Association was established in order to set rules for the game and to organize championships. The first U.S. Amateur Championship was held the next year in Newport, Rhode Island. The day after the amateur competition, the first U.S. Open was held at the same site. The winner was Horace Rawlins, who beat a field of 11 golfers to win a purse of $150. Soon thereafter, golf courses sprang up all over the country, with Chicago being the first place to have a course with 18 holes. British and American courses proved very different, for while the Scots could depend on their natural landscape for golf courses, Americans, for the most part, had to create their own landscaped courses.

In 1916, the Professional Golfers' Association (PGA) was formed. They held their first championship that year at the Siwanoy Country Club in Bronxville, New York. Golf quickly became a commercial commodity in America. Although the PGA originally only had a winter calendar, by 1944 it had a year-long calendar with 22 events. Companies sponsored golfing events and provided the prize money the athletes competed for. In turn, these companies received media attention, and the circuit became very competitive as golfers began to compete for larger purses.

Leonard de Selva/CORBIS

Men's golf clothing, circa 1926. The pants are known as "plus-fours" because of the four inches of fabric that drape over the knee.

Changes In The Game

In the beginning of the 20th century, the rubber core ball was introduced. It was lighter than its predecessor, the "gutta percha" ball, and allowed the ball to fly further. Dimples were added a few years later. By 1910, irons with grooved faces and steel-shafted clubs were introduced (the traditional hickory ones were widely used for some time, however). These changes allowed golfers to gain both distance and control over the ball. As a result, golf courses had to be expanded and made more challenging.

Americans soon became the leaders when it came to analyzing golf swings. They also led in fashion. In the 1920s, golfing attire was established in this country: plus-fours, argyle sweater vests, blazers and two-tone shoes. The British would not dress up for the game for another four decades.

In 1921, the Royal and Ancient Golf Club of St. Andrews (R&A), the governing body of European golf, limited the size and weight of the golf ball. In 1931, the USGA announced its own set of measurements. There was disagreement between the Europeans and the Americans, in part because the players had different needs. British and Scottish players who played on windy courses preferred a heavier, smaller ball.

In 1932, the R&A and USGA worked out a partial compromise on ball size, agreeing on a maximum weight of 1.62 oz, but disagreeing on minimum size (the R&A sanctioned 1.62 inches for the diameter, while the USGA set its minimum at 1.68 inches.). Today, the minimum diameter is set at 1.68 inches, except for international play, when the slightly smaller size is used. The two organizations meet every four years to go make any changes they deem necessary in the rules of the game.

The Greats

Through the years there were many advances in the technological aspect of the great game of golf that would shape the game into the sport we know today. And, along with these dramatic changes, came players who would each contribute some form of magic that would, too, help the sport advance through the years.

Born in St. Andrews, Scotland, "Old" Tom Morris was a pioneer of the sport. His first job was as an apprentice ball maker. He became a three-time winner of the British Open (1862, 1864 and 1867), though he died from injuries due to a fall he took down the stairs of the St. Andrews clubhouse in 1908.

The "Great Triumvirate" ruled golf from the late 1800s to the early 1900s. Brits John Henry Taylor and Harry Vardon, along with Scotsman James Braid, won the British Open 16 times in 20 years. In 1896, Vardon won his

Allsport Hulton Deutsch/ALLSPORT

The "Great Triumvirate," from left to right: John Henry Taylor, James Braid,
Harry Vardon. The fourth man is Sandy Herd (seated far right).

A Modern Sport

This game with modest beginnings – later usurped by royalty and the upper
classes – seems to be reaching a new age of accessibility. In 1961, the PGA
removed the "whites only" rule from its constitution and Charlie Sifford became
the first black golfer at a PGA event. Although barriers still stand – as
evidenced by the fact that some clubs withdrew from the PGA in 1990 when
it introduced further measures to end racial discrimination – Tiger Woods'
stunning career is sure to change the face of golf. He has already begun to
do so as he broadens the popularity of the sport and brings in fans from
groups that have traditionally not been participants in the sport. Today, more
than 23 million people play golf in the United States. This number is sure to
skyrocket during the reign of Tiger, golf royalty for the modern era.

first British Open (which he would go on to win a record six times). And in 1900, Vardon became the first golfer to win both the British and U.S. Opens. Vardon became golf's first international celebrity as his fame traveled across the Atlantic to the United States. He helped popularize the overlapping grip and was known for his powerful and accurate upright swing.

American Bobby Jones holds a special place as one of the greatest golfers of all time. The Atlanta native was a natural talent. Although he never had a formal lesson, his swing was smooth and strong. During his career, Jones won the British Open three times, the British Amateur once, the U.S. Open four times and the U.S. Amateur four times. He is the only golfer to have won all four of these tournaments – the original Grand Slam – in a single year, 1930. Jones never turned professional and retired from active competition at the age of 28, several months after he completed the Grand Slam.

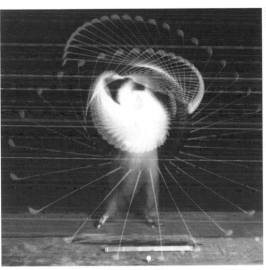

A 1938 photo of Bobby Jones displaying his driving form in 61 strobe exposures.

In the 1950s, golf teams became part of American universities, giving rise to the likes of Arnold Palmer and Jack Nicklaus. They, along with South African Gary Player, formed a second golf triumvirate – the "Big Three" – of the 1960s that would win almost every major event into the next decade. Nicklaus, "The Golden Bear," became the first professional to win all four majors and holds an unmatched record of four U.S. Open titles, six Masters and five PGA Championships.

Women On The Course

After Mary, Queen of Scots was allegedly tried for treason after playing a few rounds of golf too soon after the murder of her husband, not much was recorded about female golfers for quite some time. Then, in 1867, the first women's golf club was founded at the St. Andrews Golf Club, and in 1895, the USGA held its first women's amateur championship.

AP/WWP

The Ladies Professional Golf Association was founded in 1950, and by 1952, was holding 21 events a year. The first television coverage of an LPGA event was in 1963, helping to boost the popularity of women's golf, and by the end of the 1960s, the schedule had expanded to 34 events.

Women's golf owes much to Babe Didrikson Zaharias, an athlete who won two gold medals and a silver medal at the 1932 Olympics. She took up golf in the 1930s and, in 1947, was the first American woman to win the British Women's Open in Scotland. Over the course of her career, she won 55 pro and amateur events, including three U.S. Opens. She helped found the LPGA in 1949 and was named "Athlete of the Half Century" by the Associated Press the following year. Once, when she was asked how she

A 1932 photo of Joyce Wethered, who died in England in 1997, just one day after her 97th birthday.

was able to hit a golf ball so far, she allegedly replied, "You've got to loosen your girdle and let it rip!"

Another giant in women's golf was Joyce Wethered. She was born in England, but spent many summers in her family's house in Scotland, where she learned to play golf. She won her first English Ladies' Championship in 1920. During her nine-year career, she would win five consecutive English Ladies' Championship titles and four British Ladies titles. In 1954, she became the president of the British Ladies Golf Union.

Stiff Competition

Grand slam champion Bobby Jones once said of ladies legend Joyce Wethered, "I have never played against anyone and felt so outclassed."

Today, golf continues to evolve, and new legends add to the grand history of the sport. Tiger Woods is one such legend, and will surely go down in the annals of golf history as a great contributor to the great game of golf.

Legends Of Golf

The word "legend" is a lot like "greatest" or "best" – it's a good way to start an argument! With over 100 years of history in this country alone (and more than 500 overall), golf has seen its share of great players, in both the amateur and professional ranks.

In the following section, we'll take a look at 19 of the biggest names in golf history. We cover all the bases, from the early greats like Harry Vardon and Walter Hagen, to the legends of more recent vintage like Jack Nicklaus and Nancy Lopez. We also included the great shooters like Sam Snead, the household names like Greg Norman and the all-time record holders like Kathy Whitworth. Whether they scored a golf Grand Slam, set a record for victories or helped define the game as it is today, they've all left their mark on the links in their own way.

Players are listed alphabetically by last name (we know better than to try to rank them!) and are accompanied by their basic personal information and a brief overview of their career.

Fred Couples

Birthdate: 10/3/59
Birthplace: Seattle, WA

AP/WWP

Couples has been a fixture on the PGA tour since 1981 and is still an active player. In those 21 years, he's had 14 PGA victories, five international wins and has won one major championship. With his teammate, Davis Love III, Couples won four consecutive World Cup of Golf titles (1992-95). He also won back-to-back Vardon Trophies in 1991 and 1992.

AP/WWP

Nick
Faldo

Birthdate: 7/18/57
Birthplace: Welwyn Garden City, England

A long-time player on the PGA Tour, Faldo joined the tour in 1981 and has won numerous major championships in addition to his 34 international victories. Faldo won the 1996 Masters and donned the Green Jacket after coming back from a six-stroke deficit going into the final round.

AP/WWP

Ray
Floyd

Birthdate: 9/4/42
Birthplace: Fort Bragg, NC

North Carolina-native Ray Floyd joined the PGA Tour in 1963 and is currently active on the Senior Tour. In his career, he's won 22 PGA and 14 Senior titles, including four major championships on each tour. In 1994, the PGA named Floyd's family "Golf Family of the Year" — as his son, Robert, is currently pursuing a golf career. Floyd and Sam Snead are the only golfers to win tour events in four different decades.

George Rinhart/CORBIS

Walter
Hagen

Birthdate: 12/21/1892
Deceased: 10/5/69
Birthplace: Rochester, NY

Hagen played on the pro tour from 1913 to 1939, with 40 wins in all, including 11 major championships. Before he won the U.S. Open in 1914, Hagen planned to go to spring training with baseball's Philadelphia Nationals.

Ben
Hogan

Birthdate: 8/13/12
Deceased: 7/25/97
Birthplace: Dublin, TX

Hogan's amazing golf career spanned 40 years —
from 1931 to 1971. In those four decades, he
racked up 63 career victories and nine major
championships, perhaps none more astonishing
than his 1950 U.S. Open win. That win came only
16 months after he suffered major injuries in a
near-fatal car accident.

Bobby
Jones

Birthdate: 3/17/02
Deceased: 12/18/71
Birthplace: Atlanta, GA

One of golf's greatest legends, Bobby Jones played
the game for only 14 short years, from 1916 to
1930. In that time, he had 23 victories, 13 of them
major championships even though he was not an
official member of the PGA. He won the Grand Slam
in 1930 and retired less than two months later. Jones
couldn't stay away, however — he is one of the mas-
terminds behind the Augusta National Golf Course.

Nancy
Lopez

Birthdate: 1/6/57
Birthplace: Torrance, CA

One of the women responsible for the rising popularity of the LPGA, Nancy Lopez got off to a sizzling
start on the tour, recording nine wins her rookie
year. Since joining the tour in 1977, Lopez has
earned 45 victories and three major championships.
She is still active on the LPGA tour.

Reuters NewMedia Inc./CORBIS

Byron
Nelson

Birthdate: 2/4/12
Birthplace: Fort Worth, TX

Although he ended his career — which spanned from approximately 1932 to 1946 — with 52 victories and five major championships, perhaps Nelson's greatest year as a player was in 1945, when he won 18 of 30 U.S. tour events. Unbelievably, his winning streak included an unprecedented 11 in a row.

AP/WWP

Jack
Nicklaus

Birthdate: 1/21/40
Birthplace: Columbus, OH

Known to all as "The Golden Bear," Jack Nicklaus dominated the PGA for decades. He entered the tour in 1962 and collected 70 PGA victories, 14 international wins and 18 major championships. Today, a player on the Senior tour, Nicklaus has won 10 tournaments, 8 of those major championships. For all of his accomplishments, *GOLF Magazine* named Nicklaus their "Golfer of the Century."

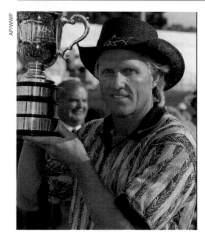

AP/WWP

Greg
Norman

Birthdate: 2/10/55
Birthplace: Mt. Isa, Queensland, Australia

The Aussie known as "The Shark" has won the Arnold Palmer Award and Vardon Trophy three times each. He joined the PGA tour in 1983 and since then has had 18 PGA and 56 international victories. In 1994, he won The Players Championship. "The Shark" is an active course architect and even has his own turf grass company!

Arnold Palmer

Birthdate: 9/10/29
Birthplace: Latrobe, PA

The man who led the PGA tour in earnings four times joined the tour in 1955 and is still active on the Senior circuit. In his years on the PGA tour, Palmer had 60 PGA victories, 13 international wins and seven major championship wins. As a Senior, he's won 10 tournaments, three of them majors.

Gary Player

Birthdate: 11/1/35
Birthplace: Johannesburg, South Africa

Player joined the PGA in 1957 and is currently on the Senior tour. Known as one of the "Big Three" (along with Palmer and Nicklaus), Player was the third golfer to win all four Grand Slam events in the course of his career. His career included 21 PGA wins, including nine majors. As a member of the Senior tour, he's already racked up 19 victories and six majors.

Nick Price

Birthdate: 1/28/57
Birthplace: Durban, South Africa

Nick Price has been on the tour since 1977, winning 16 PGA and 24 international tournaments in that time. The winner of three majors, Price has tied with Tiger Woods for most victories in the 1990s (with 15). Perhaps his biggest year was 1994, when he won both the British Open and the PGA Championship.

AP/WWP

Gene
Sarazen

Birthdate: 2/27/02
Deceased: 5/13/99
Birthplace: Harrison, NY

"The Squire," who played on the PGA tour from approximately 1920 to 1973 (that's a long career!), is credited with inventing the sand wedge. In his career, Sarazen had 38 victories and seven major championship wins. He was also the first to win all four major championships. His death in 1999 at the age of 97 was mourned throughout the golf community.

Sam
Snead

Birthdate: 5/27/12
Birthplace: Ashwood, VA

"Slammin' Sam" is the all-time leader in PGA victories with 81 wins. Snead played from approximately 1937 to 1979 and won seven major PGA championships and six major Senior championships in that time. During his career, he won the PGA Championship an astonishing four times. In 1965, Snead won the Greater Greensboro Open at the age of 52, making him the oldest player to win a PGA event.

Lee
Trevino

Birthdate: 12/1/39
Birthplace: Dallas, TX

Trevino, who has back problems from being struck by lightning during a tournament in 1975, joined the PGA tour in 1967 and is still active on the Senior tour. The self-taught player has 27 PGA and 29 Senior victories. Trevino won six majors in the PGA and has won four on the Senior tour, which he joined in 1989.

AP/WWP

Harry
Vardon*

Birthdate: 1870
Deceased: 1937
Birthplace: Grouville, Island of Jersey, Channel Islands

During a career from approximately 1890 to 1937, Vardon won over 60 tournaments, as well as six British Open victories, and got his name immortalized when the PGA named their prestigious Vardon Trophy after him. He also wrote the book on the sport — literally. His 1920s guidebook *The Gist Of Golf* is still a prized collector's item.

Tom
Watson

Birthdate: 9/4/1949
Birthplace: Kansas City, MO

Ever since coming aboard the PGA in 1971, Watson's continuing record has included 34 PGA victories and nine international wins, including an amazing 8 major championships. The PGA voted him "Player of the Year" six times before Watson moved over to the Senior PGA in 1999. In his short time there, he's already gotten two victories!

Kathy
Whitworth

Birthdate: 9/27/39
Birthplace: Monahans, TX

Whitworth proved to the world that woman can indeed do sports. Dating back to her LPGA debut in 1958, she was able to retired in 1991 after racking up an incredible 88 career victories, six of which were major championships. That's seven more than PGA record-holder Sam Snead, giving Whitworth the highest number of career wins in either association!

Tiger And The Game

The PGA

Ever since 1916, the Professional Golfers Association of America (PGA) has been bringing golf to both long-time fans and brand new spectators alike.

When a group of prominent golfers and executives met for a business luncheon at New York City's Taplow Club on January 17, 1916, they might not have realized how significant their afternoon meal would be. The meeting was planned by Rodman Wanamaker, a department store magnate who had recognized a growing trend in America. That trend was the game of golf. Wanamaker was willing to bankroll a golf organization and finance the first American golf tournament for professionals. A few months later, their organization would be formally introduced as the Professional Golfers Association of America.

From Pastime To Professional Sport

Brought to North American shores by Scottish immigrants, golf's popularity had been growing for years. Yet hardly anyone regarded it as a sport. To most people, golf was just a game for amateurs and those who played it professionally were hardly more than employees at the clubs. But Wanamaker saw golf's potential to become a widespread American pastime, and understood it to be far more than just a rich man's diversion.

The PGA was America's first organization for golf professionals. It was designed to help to further public interest in golf, promote tournaments

Gary Newkirk/AllSport

The PGA Championship trophy is named for PGA founder Rodman Wanamaker.

for professionals and, above all, allow golf to be recognized as a legitimate sport. Since that memorable lunch meeting, the PGA has grown into the largest professional sports organization in the United States. Boasting

over 20,000 employees, the association promotes an annual series of tournaments, runs golf schools and presents the most coveted awards in the game. But, since its small-time start, the PGA's goals and objectives haven't changed a bit.

On Tour

When the newly formed PGA decided to sponsor a tour for professional golfers, they had no way of knowing that it would someday be as successful as it has since become. But, almost a century later, the PGA tour has grown into one of the largest money makers in modern sports, with purses for the

Payne Stewart swings at the ball during the last round of the 1995 PGA Championship, held at the Riviera Country Club in Los Angeles.

victors reaching well into the millions. It's come a long way from professionals just trying to make a living!

These days, the PGA tour hosts nearly 50 golfing tournaments held throughout the country which are now witnessed by millions of people. It's not easy to become a player, however. Getting onto the tour requires some serious work.

Some of the tour members have earned their position by sponsor exemptions. Sponsors finance their way into a few select tournaments, and if they manage to win enough money to make the list of the 125 highest-paid players, they're automatically guaranteed a spot on the tour. That's how it worked for Tiger Woods.

But if you haven't proved that you're a rising star, you'll have to enter the PGA Qualifying School, which is a fairly hard route. Commonly called "Q School," it's a grueling, one-week boot camp for future golf professionals. Up to 1,000 students may enter but few will emerge with their scores – and their egos – in top shape. Surviving Q School earns the graduate a player's card, and the right to compete in the following year's PGA tour. It's a difficult task, but it's worth it in the long run.

Footing The Bill

It takes money to play at all those gorgeous clubs and courses. To finance the tour's individual events, the PGA has partnered with some of the most prestigious and profitable corporations in the world. Lucrative businesses like AT&T and Sony sponsor individual tournaments all over the country. Sometimes, a company will sponsor a specific part of each tournament, like the scoreboards, which are provided by IBM, MasterCard and Charles Schwab.

David Morland visually follows the ball after his tee-off at the 2000 PGA Qualifying Tournament.

Taking Something Home

The annual PGA Tour isn't just about winning individual tournaments. Each year, the individual players' performances make them eligible for one of two elite golf teams.

To qualify for the Ryder Cup Matches, a player must earn points based on his rankings in individual tournaments during the course of two PGA seasons. Accumulation of these points always begins with the first tour of even-numbered years and ends with the PGA Championship the following year. For instance, rankings for the 2001 Ryder Cup Matches began on January 9, 2000 and ended with the completion of the PGA Championship on August 19, 2001. The ten players with the most accumulated points at the end of this time period, plus two player's selected by the team's captain, compete as part of the American Team for the Ryder Cup.

The European Team is chosen much the same way, except that points are based on money earned during the season. Rankings for the 2001 Ryder Cup

Vijay Singh, winner of the 2000 Masters Tournament, chips on the third hole of the President's Cup Tournament on October 19, 2000.

European Team began on September 10, 2000 and ended at the conclusion of the BMW European Open in August 2001.

In non-Ryder Cup years, a PGA player's individual earnings for the tour can get him a spot on the U.S. Team for the President's Cup. The 15 highest paid players get to compete against their world counterparts on the International Team, who are chosen on the basis of the Official World Golf rankings, for the President's Cup. Players eligible for the European Ryder Cup Team are exempt from taking part in this tournament.

Local Act

In a country this large, it would be impossible for one organization to keep track of the numerous golfers who play professionally! The PGA is actually made of up 41 different "Section Offices," each of which corresponds to a specific region of the United States. The head office of each section holds regional tryouts for amateur golfers, and seeks to stir up interest in golf among as many people as possible. So, if you're interested in trying to become a member of the PGA, or just want to improve your golfing abilities, your local section is definitely the place to visit.

Tiger Woods discusses his golf clinic with the press.

Phil Cole/AllSport

School's In Session

Golf champions aren't born. They have to put in long hours of practice and training, sometimes for many years. And once they've made it to the top, they've certainly earned the title of professional golfer!

Kirk Triplett discusses the mechanics of golf to a group of novice golfers.

But even if you don't plan on going pro any time soon, the PGA is still there to help you. So, whether you're a 20-year-veteran of the links or a newcomer who doesn't know a 5-iron from the back nine, there's hope for you in Port St. Lucie, Florida.

That's where you'll find the PGA Learning Center, a place where you'll get an education unlike any other. Have you ever wanted to improve your swing or learn how to get out of a bunker without digging a hole big enough to crawl and hide your embarrassment? The school features courses

Learning The Course

The PGA Learning Center features four distinct courses: the Fazio North Course, the Fazio South Course, the private PGA Country Club and the Dye Course.

that re-create a variety of designs and even clinics to help you work on specific maneuvers. Plus, all of the teachers are dedicated and qualified PGA professionals who have been actively pursuing the game for years and have seen it all.

The center offers courses for women and seniors, also. You can even sign up for a couple's lesson and take to the course with your sweetie for a relaxing day out on the links learning from the best instructors the game has to offer. Whether you sign up for a day of instruction or an intense three-day course of study, you'll be driving and putting with the best in the business. Courses cover every topic imaginable, from mental preparedness and equipment tutorials to an analysis of your swing.

A League Of Their Own

When you watch a major golf tournament, you'll notice that all the players are men. Before you worry about discrimination, you should know that women golfers have an association too, and the Ladies Professional Golfers Association (LPGA) is every bit as popular and competitive as the men's version. In fact, it's been that way for half a century.

After the Women's Professional Golf Association folded for financial reasons in 1949, a number of female professional golfers decided that they weren't going to give up playing professionally. Twelve of the most respected women in golf – including the legendary Babe Didrikson Zaharias and Louise Suggs – met in 1950 to lay the foundation for the LPGA. During that first year, golf fans were astonished to see 14 tournaments for women, all of which were run by the professionals themselves. Having very little money at this early point, the golfers couldn't hire any employees yet!

For Girls Only

The LPGA's goals also include introducing golf to young girls everywhere, which they do through scholarship programs and their LPGA Girls Golf Club. During one season, the LPGA will host 40 tournaments nationwide, some of which can be seen on television's Golf Channel.

Mi Hyun Kim tees off in the First Union Betsy King Classic in October 1999. She won the 72-hole event with a score of 8-under 280.

Today, the LPGA stands as the oldest women's professional sports or ganization in the world. It's a non-profit organization now, with a strong dedication to worthy charities. Through the LPGA Foundation, the organization provides scholarships, runs youth programs and gives financial assistance to several charities as well as to individuals in the golf industry who experience financial hardships.

Never Too Young . . .

Kevin Smith, a 4-year-old golfer, prepares to compete in the U.S. Kids Golf World Championship.

Since a big part of the PGA's focus is to promote golf among the general public, the organization has always made an effort to reach out to young people and introduce them to a new and exciting sport. If they start early enough, they may move on to bigger and brighter things, such as the PGA Junior Series.

Since the summer of 1996, the PGA has organized a two-month series of tournaments for youths between the ages of 13 and 17, both boys and girls. To date, over 8,000 youngsters have taken to the links and shown the world that golf talent doesn't recognize any age difference!

A Different Kind Of Swing

The PGA started the "First Swing" program, a program which works in conjunction with schools and other sports clubs to get kids started in golf at an early age.

. . . Or Too Old

In many sports, you would expect any athlete over the age of 50 to be washed up. Could someone of that age be expected to execute a tackle in football, or slam-dunk a basketball?

But that's not the case with golf. According to veteran golfer Bruce Fleisher, "At the age of 50, if you can't have fun playing the game you've loved and wanted to play your whole life, then something is wrong." For professional golfers over the age of 50, there's no reason to retire. The Senior PGA Tour has been part of the PGA since 1980, when the organization was

> "If it is your lifelong passion, you can't imagine not being part of it. I might be like Arnie, play until I'm 70."
>
> Tiger Woods

established as a tour for golf's top scoring professionals. That made it a golf equivalent of an All-Star game, showcasing golf's best career players who still have the skills to birdie their way to the top. The Senior PGA tour players now compete for the Charles Schwab Cup, awarded to the player who wins the most money over the course of the season. It's always a close battle to take that cup home!

Hale Irwin celebrates a victory at the 2000 U.S. Senior Open, held in Bethlehem, Pennsylvania.

PGA Courses

Golfers on the PGA tour can look forward to taking on some of the greatest courses in the game. Here's a look at the tour's stops for the 2001 season. Please note that some tournaments are played on more than one course.

Annandale Golf Club
Madison, Mississippi
Southern Farm Bureau Classic

Par 72 • 7,157 Yards

The 1999 event was shortened to 54 holes so players could attend Payne Stewart's funeral.

Atlanta Athletic Club (Highlands Course)
Duluth, Georgia
PGA Championship

Par 70 • 7,213 Yards

The Highlands Course was redesigned in 1995.

Augusta National Golf Club
Augusta, Georgia
The Masters Tournament

Par 72 • 6,985 Yards

After the first tournament in 1934, the order in which the nines were played was reversed.

Bay Hill Club & Lodge
Orlando, Florida
Bay Hill Invitational

Par 72 • 7,207 Yards

As president of the Club, Arnold Palmer can often be seen on the course or in one of the Club's dining rooms!

The Belfry (The Brabazon Course)
Sutton, England
The Ryder Cup

Par 72 • 7,118 Yards

Tiger Woods was the first to clinch a 2001 U.S. Ryder Cup team berth.

Bellerive Country Club
St. Louis, Missouri
World Golf Championships - American Express Championship

Par 71 • 7,177 Yards

Voted 53rd on *GolfWeb's* list of "100 Greatest Golf Courses in the U.S."

Bermuda Dunes Country Club
Bermuda Dunes, California
Bob Hope Chrysler Classic

Par 72 • 6,927 Yards

The course has hosted the Bob Hope Chrysler Classic since its inception 42 years ago.

Brown Deer Park Golf Course
Milwaukee, Wisconsin
Greater Milwaukee Open

Par 71 • 6,739 Yards

Tiger Woods' first pro start was at the GMO in 1996. He finished tied for 60th.

Callaway Gardens Resort (Mountain View Course)
Pine Mountain, Georgia
Buick Challenge

Par 72 • 7,057 Yards

The 15th hole is one of the more difficult par-5 holes on the PGA tour.

Castle Pines Golf Club
Castle Rock, Colorado
The International

Par 72 • 7,559 Yards

Golfers can find a veritable wildlife reserve on the course; including elk, bobcats, hawks and prairie dogs.

Champions Golf Club (Cypress Creek Course)
Houston, Texas
The Tour Championship

Par 71 • 7,200 Yards

Ranked #2 on the Texas Golf Network's "Top 20 Courses In The State."

Cog Hill Golf & Country Club ("Dubsdread")
Lemont, Illinois
Advil Western Open

Par 72 • 7,086 Yards

Nicknamed "Dubsdread" ("dubbers beware") after a Florida golf course.

Colonial Country Club
Fort Worth, Texas
Mastercard Colonial

Par 70 • 7,010 Yards

In a 2001 *TravelGolf.com* article, Curtis Strange called Colonial "one of the great golf courses in the world."

Desert Inn Golf Club
Las Vegas, Nevada
Invensys Classic

Par 72 • 7,193 Yards

The Desert Inn Golf Club is the only championship course on the Las Vegas Strip.

Nick Faldo (in green shirt) watches John Daly tee off on the 18th hole at Augusta National Golf Club.

Many a golfer has landed in the 11th-hole bunker at TPC at Sawgrass in Florida.

Doral Golf Resort & Spa (Blue Course)
Miami, Florida
Doral-Ryder Open
Genuity Championship

Par 72 • 6,701 Yards

Nicknamed the "Blue Monster."

English Turn Golf & Country Club
New Orleans, Louisiana
COMPAQ Classic

Par 72 • 7,078 Yards

English Turn's 18th hole is one of the more difficult on the PGA tour.

En-Joie Golf Club
Endicott, New York
B.C. Open

Par 72 • 6,974 Yards

The course was completely renovated in 1996, including expansion of the greens and installation of traps.

Firestone Country Club (South Course)
Akron, Ohio
World Golf Championships – NEC Invitational

Par 70 • 7,149 Yards

Redesigned by Robert Trent Jones, Sr.

Forest Oaks Country Club
Greensboro, North Carolina
Greater Greensboro Chrysler Classic

Par 72 • 7,062 Yards

The Greater Greensboro Chrysler Classic dates to 1938, making it the third-oldest tournament on the tour.

Four Seasons – Cottonwood Valley Country Club
Irving, Texas
GTE Byron Nelson Classic

Par 71 • 6,927 Yards

Cottonwood's first hole has a green shaped like Texas.

Four Seasons - TPC at Las Colinas
Irving, Texas
GTE Byron Nelson Classic

Par 70 • 6,899 Yards

The 17th hole is very difficult, as it is open to blustery winds.

Harbour Town Golf Links
Hilton Head Island, South Carolina
WorldCom Classic –
The Heritage of Golf

Par 71 • 6,973 Yards

Players use the Harbour Town Lighthouse to line up 18th hole shots.

Indian Wells Country Club
Indian Wells, California
Bob Hope Chrysler Classic

Par 72 • 6,479 Yards

This course is famous for low scores – three of the four 61s in the event's history have been shot here.

Kingsmill Golf Club (River Course)
Williamsburg, Virginia
Michelob Championship at Kingsmill

Par 71 • 6,797 Yards

Fans in "Curtis Strange's Navy" watch the 17th from the James River.

La Cantera Golf Club
San Antonio, Texas
Westin Texas Open at La Cantera

Par 72 • 7,001 Yards

La Cantera hosted Tiger Woods at the Texas Open in 1996. Woods finished third at -11, 277.

La Quinta Country Club
La Quinta, California
Bob Hope Chrysler Classic

Par 72 • 7,060 Yards

This course has hosted the Classic since 1964 and rotates with Tamarisk Country Club.

Laurel Valley Country Club
Ligonier, Pennsylvania
Marconi Pennsylvania Classic

Par 71 • 7,066 Yards

Tiger Woods graced Laurel Valley for a benefit skins game in August 1997.

Metropolitan Golf Club
Melbourne, Australia
World Golf Championships –
Accenture Match Play Championship

Par 72 • 7,066 Yards

Greg Norman described the fairways as the best he had ever played on.

Montreux Golf & Country Club
Reno, Nevada
Reno-Tahoe Open

Par 72 • 7,552 Yards

"The Golden Bear" hole is named after Montreux's legendary architect – golfing great Jack Nicklaus.

Muirfield Village Golf Club
Dublin, Ohio
Memorial Tournament

Par 72 • 7,193 Yards

The late Payne Stewart will be honored at the 2001 Memorial Tournament at Muirfield, May 28 to June 3.

Northview Golf & Country Club (Ridge Course)
Surrey, British Columbia, Canada
Air Canada Championship

Par 72 • 6,900 Yards

A dogleg approach to the green makes the third hole very challenging.

Omni Tucson National Golf Resort & Spa
Tucson, Arizona
Touchstone Energy Tucson Open

Par 72 • 7,148 Yards

The resort actually has three separate nine-hole courses.

Pebble Beach Golf Links
Pebble Beach, California
AT&T Pebble Beach National Pro-Am

Par 72 • 6,799 Yards

Voted the #1 golf course in *Golf Digest*'s 2001 list of "America's 100 Greatest Golf Courses."

PGA West (Arnold Palmer Course)
La Quinta, California
Bob Hope Chrysler Classic

Par 72 • 6,474 Yards

PGA West includes five other courses.

The Plantation Course at Kapalua Resort
Kapalua, Hawaii
Mercedes Championships

Par 73 • 7,263 Yards

The Mercedes Championship is held at the Plantation Course every year.

Poppy Hills
Pebble Beach, California
AT&T Pebble Beach National Pro-Am

Par 72 • 6,833 Yards

Home of the Northern California Golf Association.

Riviera Country Club
Pacific Palisades, California
Nissan Open

Par 71 • 6,950 Yards

Hosted the U.S. Open in 1948; PGA Championship in 1983 and 1995; the U.S. Senior Open in 1998.

Royal Lytham & St. Anne's Golf Club
Lytham St. Anne's, Lancashire, England
British Open

Par 71 • 6,723 Yards

Has hosted the British Open 10 times.

Royal Montreal Golf Club (Blue Course)
Montreal, Quebec, Canada
Bell Canadian Open

Par 70 • 6,797 Yards

Features water hazards on six of the final nine holes.

Southern Highlands Golf Club
Las Vegas, Nevada
Invensys Classic

Par 72 • 7,381 Yards

One of only three courses worldwide co-designed by Robert Trent Jones, Sr. and Jr.

Tony Roberts/CORBIS

Perils galore await on Southern Hills Country Club's 13th hole.

Southern Hills Country Club
Tulsa, Oklahoma
U.S. Open Championship

Par 70 • 6,834 Yards

The challenging Southern Hills features 10 doglegged holes.

Spyglass Hill Golf Course
Pebble Beach, California
AT&T Pebble Beach National Pro-Am

Par: 72 • 6,855 Yards

The course's name and hole names come from Robert Louis Stevenson's novel, *Treasure Island.*

Taiheiyo Club Gotemba Course
Gotemba, Japan
WGC-EMC World Cup

Par 72 • 7,072 Yards

The view from this course includes the majestic Mt. Fuji.

TPC at Avenel
Potomac, Maryland
Kemper Insurance Open

Par 71 • 7,005 Yards

Arnold Palmer won the inaugural KIO in 1968.

TPC at Deere Run
Silvis, Illinois
John Deere Classic

Par 71 • 7,138 Yards

The 16th is named "Mother Earth" for the Native Americans who lived on the site as many as 5,000 years ago.

TPC at Heron Bay
Coral Springs, Florida
The Honda Classic

Par 72 • 7,268 Yards

TPC made *Golf Magazine*'s "Top Ten Public Golf Courses You Can Play."

TPC at River Highlands
Cromwell, Connecticut
Canon Greater Hartford Open

Par 70 • 6,820 Yards

TPC at River Highlands has seen several design and name changes over the years, most recently in 1991.

TPC at Sawgrass
Ponte Vedra Beach, Florida
The Players Championship

Par 72 • 6,937 Yards

The infamous 17th hole is an island of danger – literally!

Tournament Players Club at Scottsdale
Scottsdale, Arizona
Phoenix Open

Par 71 • 7,088 Yards

The 16th hole is famous for a Tiger Woods hole-in-one in 1998.

TPC at Southwind
Memphis, Tennessee
FedEx St. Jude Classic

Water hazards are a common (and frustrating!) feature of the TPC at Southwind.

TPC at Summerlin
Las Vegas, Nevada
Invensys Classic

Par 72 • 7,243 Yards

Tiger Woods earned his first PGA tour victory at TPC at Summerlin in 1996 at the Las Vegas Invitational.

TPC at Sugarloaf
Duluth, Georgia
BellSouth Classic

Par 72 • 7,259 Yards

In 1998, tornadoes destroyed many trees on the course but repairs were made before the BellSouth Classic.

Tony Roberts/CORBIS

Sunlight glitters off the Pacific Ocean at the 6th hole of Torrey Pines' North Course.

TPC at The Woodlands
The Woodlands, Texas
Shell Houston Open

Par 72 • 7,042 Yards

The water hazard at the 17th hole is nicknamed "Devil's Bathtub."

Torrey Pines Golf Course (North Course)
La Jolla, California
Buick Invitational

Par 72 • 6,874 Yards

A particularly challenging course thanks to its many bunkers.

Torrey Pines Golf Course (South Course)
La Jolla, California
Buick Invitational

Par 72 • 7,055 Yards

Tiger Woods holds the South Course record of 62 (1999).

Waialae Country Club
Honolulu, Hawaii
Sony Open

Par 72 • 7,012 Yards

Some scenes from the movie *From Here to Eternity* were filmed at this beautiful course.

Walt Disney World Resort (Magnolia)
Lake Buena Vista, Florida
National Car Rental Golf Classic

Par 72 • 7,190 Yards

The third and fourth rounds are played on the Magnolia course.

Walt Disney World Resort (Palm)
Lake Buena Vista, Florida
National Car Rental Golf Classic

Par 72 • 6,957 Yards

Tiger Woods won the 1999 National Car Rental Golf Classic by a stroke.

Warwick Hills Golf & Country Club
Grand Blanc, Michigan
Buick Open

Par 72 • 7,105 Yards

Tiger Woods' best finish in the Buick Open to date: -13, 275, tied for 4th.

The Westin Innisbrook Resort (Copperhead Course)
Palm Harbor, Florida
Tampa Bay Classic

Par 72 • 7,086 Yards

This course hosts the relatively new Tampa Bay Classic every year.

Tony Roberts/CORBIS

Harbour Town Golf Links' 16th hole.

Other Great Courses

In addition to the courses on the schedule for 2001, the PGA makes frequent stops at some other great venues. Chief among these is the **The Old Course** at St. Andrews, Scotland, whose rugged terrain and glorious tradition combine for a thrilling golf experience. History reigns at The Old Course, from the Road Hole through Hell Bunker to the Royal & Ancient Golf Club off the 18th. Golfers can find serene beauty at **Poipu Bay Golf Course,** home of the PGA's Grand Slam of Golf since 1994. Nestled on 80-foot cliffs on the Hawaiian island of Kauai, Poipui offers spectacular views of blue water and ancient stone ruins. Back on the mainland, **Shinnecock Hills Golf Club** in Southampton, New York, stands as one of the oldest courses in the United States. Built in 1891, par-70 course is noted for its fast greens and often tricky winds. The U.S. Open will return to Shinnecock in 2004.

Just as challenging is **Winged Foot Golf Club** in Mamaroneck, New York. A frequent U.S. Open and PGA Championship stop, Winged Foot is one of the least forgiving courses on the tour. Hale Irwin's 1974 U.S. Open win at a +7, 287 is an extreme example of the difficulties that await even the tour's best golfers. **Inverness Country Club** in Toledo, Ohio, is also a highly respected PGA stop. The 7,255-yard course has hosted the greats in the game, from Byron Nelson to Jack Nicklaus, who played in his first major at Inverness as an amateur in 1957.

The 15th green at Shinnecock, seen from the tee.

Tiger's Challengers

With his awesome skills and magnetic personality, there is no other golfer quite like Tiger Woods. However, the PGA is filled with many other golfers who equal Tiger in both aptitude and appeal. Whether you're talking on the green or off, these great players are there, each contributing their own unique talent to the field of men's golf.

David Duval

David Duval follows his tee-off drive at the 2001 AT&T Pebble Beach National Pro-Am.

As one of the premier players under the age of 30 on the tour, David Duval has the youthful stamina to remain a legitimate challenger to Tiger for years to come. In 2000, Duval won the 12th tour of his career, placing him squarely in the company of other young greats such as Tiger and Phil Mickelson. In 1999, Duval reached a career pinnacle by climbing to the top of the golf rankings. Duval's charge to the top broke Tiger's amazing streak of being ranked the top golfer in the world, marking the first time in 41 weeks that Tiger hadn't been at the top of the chart. These rivals of the green joined forces in 2000, bringing home a victory for the United States as teammates in the World Cup of Golf tournament in Argentina. Whether playing on the same team or against each other, Tiger and Duval continue to bring out the best in each other on the golf course.

Ernie Els

One of life's sad facts is that no one ever remembers second place. From silver medalists in the Olympics to last year's Super Bowl runner-up, much of the glory of athletic competition is reserved for the winners.

It might seem like Ernie Els has been stuck in the shadow of Tiger Woods, but the South African golfer, nicknamed "Big Easy," has become quite a large presence on the course, in spite of Tiger's dominance. During a hot 2000 season in which he posted the best numbers of his career, Els found that Tiger was the one man he could not beat that millennial year. Els had two second-place finishes behind Tiger, including a heartbreaking finish in the Mercedes Championships, where he eventually fell short to Tiger on the second sudden-death playoff hole. That loss was just the most recent in a string of wrenching losses to Tiger. At the Johnnie Walker Classic in Thailand in 1998, Els fell victim to the second-place slump when Woods came back from eight shots to overtake Els for the win. Els had better luck against Tiger in 1999, however, when he beat him by two strokes at the Nissan Open. As Els con-

Ernie Els tips his hat to the gallery after sinking a putt on the 18th green in the quarterfinals of the 2001 World Match Play Golf Championships in Melbourne, Australia.

tinues to improve, all signs indicate that he will soon step out of the shadows and into the spotlight in the golfing world.

Sergio Garcia

He's young. He's personable. He's an amazing golfer. And his name isn't Tiger Woods.

21-year-old Sergio Garcia's remarkable play has the golf world showering praise on this Spanish star nicknamed "El Niño." In just his second year on the PGA Tour, Garcia defeated Tiger (before a nationally televised audience, no less) during a one-on-one matchup known as the "Battle at Bighorn" in August of 2000.

Sergio Garcia flashes a smile on the practice green at the 2001 Masters in Augusta, Georgia.

Garcia also had a memorable battle with Tiger in 1999, when he stood his ground during the final three holes at the PGA Championship. The young Spaniard's shot on the 16th hole almost landed in a tree, but Garcia closed his eyes and smacked it out of the rough and onto the green. And though he didn't overtake Tiger, his second-place finish and exuberance on the course earned him plenty of attention. Now all eyes are set on Garcia as he prepares to emerge as a worthy challenger to Tiger.

Davis Love III takes a swing in the final round of the 2001 Buick Invitational in San Diego.

Davis Love III

Davis Love III's consistency paid off in spades in 2000 when he briefly held the first-place ranking on the PGA tour career money list, passing Greg Norman. In his last six seasons, Love has earned at least $1 million in earnings each year. Who passed Love to claim the #1 earnings spot? It was none other than Tiger Woods!

Love finished directly behind Tiger at the Bay Hill Invitational in 2000. In 1996, Love also fell short to Tiger at the Las Vegas Invitational. Tiger's victory in Las Vegas that year won him his first PGA tour title. As one of the top money earners in the game, Love would probably love nothing better to earn the distinction of beating Tiger Woods.

Phil Mickelson

When Tiger Woods gets on a roll, competitors have been known to roll over as if they were playing dead. Never one to lie down without a fight, Phil Mickelson is one of the few golfers who can say that they put the "tiger" back in its cage. Mickelson breezed to victory over Tiger by four strokes at the Buick Invitational in 2000, ending Tiger's string of six consecutive victories. But Tiger has shown in the past that he can handle Mickelson. In 1999, Tiger was a winner by one stroke over Mickelson at the World Golf

Championships-NEC Invitational. That victory made up for a defeat Tiger suffered to Mickelson at the Mercedes Championships in 1998.

Mickelson and Tiger (along with golf legend Jack Nicklaus) are the only golfers to win the NCAA Championship and the U.S. Amateur in the same year. Tiger and Mickelson are amateurs no longer, and their memorable battles on the pro tour have left fans anxiously awaiting their next meeting.

A determined Phil Mickelson drives off the ninth tee in the third round of the 2001 Masters.

Vijay Singh

"V for victory" is an apt phrase to describe Vijay Singh, whose name is a Hindi word meaning "victory." Vijay's been golfing professionally since 1982, but his recent victories show he is only now beginning to hit his stride. He donned his first Green Jacket after winning the Masters at Augusta in 2000 (the missing link to a "true" Grand Slam for Tiger). Also in 2000, Tiger edged out Vijay at the PGA Grand Slam of Golf when he eagled the 18th hole to tie Vijay, and then took the win with an eagle in the sudden-death tiebreaker. It was the second time Tiger edged out Vijay at the event, the first time coming

in 1998 when Vijay lost his lead after bogeying three times in a row.

There seemed to be a bit of a rivalry between the two during the 2000 Presidents Cup competition. Both men refused to concede putts for the other, and during the event Vijay's caddie had "Tiger Who?" emblazoned on his cap. But with his recent level of play, you can be sure no one is asking "Vijay Who?" any longer.

Defending champ Vijay Singh looks pensive as he waits to tee off during a practice round at the 2001 Masters.

Great LPGA Players Of Today

Just as Tiger Woods has rewritten the record books of the PGA, there are several women currently playing in the LPGA that have exhibited their own amazing displays of sportsmanship and talent.

While at times it seems as if there is no legitimate challenger to Tiger Woods's supremacy in the world of men's golf, there is no shortage of ultra-competitive, talented women in the Ladies Professional Golf Association.

The three women currently demolishing the LPGA record books are an international mix from all corners of the globe. Annika Sorenstam, Se Ri Pak and Karrie Webb are all destined to become household names as the LPGA continues to rise in popularity.

South Korea's Se Ri Pak tees off during the final round of the 2001 YourLife Vitamins LPGA Classic.

AP/WWP

Se Ri Pak is one of the younger superstars of the LPGA, but she has already earned over $2 million in her four years on the tour. In her native South Korea, Pak won dozens of golf tournaments before setting her sights on America. Since moving to the United States in 1997, she secured eight victories in her first two seasons and was named Rookie of the Year in 1998. While she has since cooled from that blazing pace, Pak has continuously managed to finish in

the top ten and the young golfer has already managed to add two victories in 2001 to her impressive list of accomplishments.

Annika Sorenstam hails from Sweden, and has given Karrie Webb several memorable head-to-head matchups throughout the years. Sorenstam is only the third player in LPGA history to win four events in a row, a feet which she accomplished in 2001. Her record-tying fourth win saw her erase a 10-stroke deficit in what became the greatest come-from-behind victory in LPGA history. In 2001, Sorenstam set records by finish-

Annika Sorenstam sets up on the 18th green at the 1997 Hawaiian Ladies Open.

ing a tournament with a final score of 27 under par on a 72-hole course. She also shot a 59 in the second round of the Standard Register PING tournament, a score that has rarely been equalled in either men's or women's golf.

Australian-born **Karrie Webb** often hears her name mentioned in the same breath as Tiger Woods. It has even been suggested that Webb and Woods square off in an all-star competition. Although that has yet to happen, Webb seems determined to keep pace with Tiger in the win column. And now, with over 20 LPGA victories to her credit, Webb has secured a spot in the LPGA Tour Hall of Fame. However, don't plan for a party just yet; Webb is indeed a golfer ahead of her time and is not officially eligible for induction until the end of the 2005 season.

Karrie Webb displays a new addition to her trophy shelf at the Du Maurier Classic.

World Wide Webb

In addition to her success on American golf courses, Karrie Webb has won the Australian Open and the Nichirei Championship on the Japanese LPGA Tour.

A Fan-tastic Sport

The Tournament Day Experience

Although it's never as rowdy as football or as fast-paced as basketball, golf is still a very popular spectator sport in America. Fans of the pastime pride themselves on being a little different than your average sports enthusiasts. Actually, watching golf is almost a sport of its own. At the least, it's very good exercise.

Buying Tickets

Granted, some tickets to major tournaments can be pricey, but there are tickets available for everyone, from every walk of life and every level of interest. The first step to attending a golf event is choosing which tournament is most convenient for you, or which one fascinates you the most. Whether you're planning to travel abroad to watch the Ryder Cup Matches or you're just going to grab a stool and park yourself in the gallery of a local PGA event, the process of purchasing tickets and preparing for a day (or more!) on the green is fairly standard across the board.

Thanks to the dawn of the "Internet Age," buying tickets for golf tourneys is a snap, that is, if you click on-line fast enough. Most tickets can be purchased either for an entire tournament or just for individual days. For

Golf fans are finding new, creative ways to show their support for Tiger Woods.

example, during the PGA Championship Tournament, you can walk the course all seven days for approximately $200. For just about $100 more, you can purchase a week-long pass to the green and the clubhouse pavilion. If you only want to be out in the sun practicing your golf clap for an afternoon, you can spend anywhere between $25 and $75 on a "Daily Grounds Ticket," depending on which day you plan to attend. Other tournaments, such as the Masters, have closed patron lists for tickets (which means that only those people on the list can purchase tickets), or might require you to submit a formal application to attend any of that week's events.

Free Parking

If you plan on going to the Masters event in Augusta, Georgia, don't worry about paying for parking. You can park for free on a first-come, first-serve basis in specified areas of the grounds as long as it's available. Additional parking areas will be assigned, but you might have a bit of a walk back to your car at the end of the day.

However, even if tickets for the main events are sold out or closed, practice-round tickets might still be available. Practice rounds are often less formal than the tournament itself, and some people actually prefer to attend

AP/WWP

Fans stretch with anticipation to see where the ball landed after Tiger maneuvered it out of the rough onto the 18th fairway of the 2000 Buick Open.

Fans set out at daybreak to stake their claim to a spot around the ninth hole of the 2001 Masters.

AP/WWP

the pre-tournament events to get a "slice" of what it's really like to be a professional golfer. These tickets, too, can be limited in number, so it's always best to plan in advance and be prepared for any situation.

Mind Your P's and Q's

Coming across tickets for a major event can be complicated, and for first-time gallery members (spectators are known as "the gallery"), keeping track of the many written and unwritten rules of golf etiquette can often be just as confusing. However, if you keep in mind a few basic concepts about the game of golf, everything else should fall into place.

The golfer's concentration is of the utmost importance. Complete silence is required while a golfer is preparing his swing. Certainly, carrying on, loud cheering, or any pre-swing vocal encouragement from the gallery is frowned upon. After a golfer has finished his shot, a measured amount of murmuring and clapping is acceptable. One will never witness fans breaking out into "the wave" or expressing jubilation in any way other than a respectful, metered clap. You will be told by the course marshal when it is time to cease all applause or conversation and prepare for the next golfer.

Websites For The Major Events

www.masters.org
www.pga.com
www.opengolf.com
www.usopen.com

It's also advised to leave your cell phones and pagers at home. Check the course regulations before you go, because some tournaments, such as the

Masters, actually ban cell phones. If they are permitted, and you must have them on your person, it's understood that they will be turned to silent mode or will remain off throughout the day.

Much More Than "A Good Walk Spoiled"

As a member of the gallery, you have a few spectating options. Many onlookers prefer to walk the entire course with the golfer they're most interested in, even if it means traveling what could amount to a four-mile walk on a hot and humid summer afternoon. To make sure that you don't miss your favorites, pick up a pairings sheet at the beginning of the day to see when each golfer will be teeing off.

If you're not particularly interested in any one player, you can wander at your leisure from hole to hole and watch different groups play through. Or you can camp out at a location of your choosing and wait for the sport to come to you. Many people say that being at any location at a golf course means you're missing a lot of action just about everywhere else. Once you've come

When it rains, it pours. Golf fans carry their coordinating umbrellas to keep dry while trekking between holes during the Masters' practice round in Augusta in April 2001.

to terms with the fact that you can't see everything there is to see in one afternoon, you'll be a much more relaxed spectator and you'll likely enjoy your afternoon far more.

Even though you can't be at every hole at once, you don't have to miss out on any of the tournament action. Scoreboards are posted around the course to update the spectators on the latest standings.

You might not know which viewing strategy suits you and your party best, so make sure you pack a stool, or some other type of lawn chair that's not too bulky, distracting or difficult to transport. Sometimes, bleachers are available for spectators.

As with everything else in golf, there is a certain way to travel the course. First, be sure to follow the ropes and stay behind them at all times. You may

Lights, No Camera, Action

Spectators are not allowed to take photos on the golf course (except during practice rounds) because they tend to create a distraction. So, don't plan on taking any group pictures of you and Tiger Woods after his round. The press are the only people authorized to take photographs during a match.

The gallery crowds the ropes on the path to the sixth hole during the final round of the 1997 Masters where Tiger would claim his first Masters Tournament victory.

Johnathan Ferry/AllSport

Though some might think this fan is a distraction on the course, he's one of many Tiger fans that have changed the way people perceive golf. There's no doubt who he's rooting for!

cross the fairway, but do so only at marked crosswalks. And if you think that at any time your moving about on the course might be a distraction to a player or an official, be considerate and wait for a more opportune time to get from point A to point B.

Dressed For Success

Yes, what you wear is important. Players have certain dress code restrictions, and so does the gallery. However, there's more to preparing for the day than carefully considering your wardrobe – you need to come prepared for the weather and for what might amount to a very long walk in the sun. Now, do you want to be lugging anything unnecessary with you? Probably not.

Traditional golf attire includes a collared shirt and pants. Yes, a tank top and shorts would most likely be the most comfortable outfit (and most convenient for working on your tan), but it's best to check the course guidelines to be absolutely certain you're dressed properly. Just because there's a sandtrap nearby doesn't mean you should be dressed for the beach.

Also, be sure to check the weather so you know whether to bring an extra bottle of sunscreen or to pack an umbrella. There's not a lot of shade near the green, so you might also want to consider wearing a hat and bringing sunglasses. After all you don't want to miss the action due to sun glare!

Miss Manners' Guide To The Masters

According to the Masters Tournament publication, "The Masters Tournament patrons know their golf and they respect golf gallery etiquette. They expect to see the game at its best and regularly show every courtesy to the players and to one another."

Getting An Autograph, Or Three, Or Fore!

Feel free to pack a pen and some of your favorite golf memorabilia, or maybe just a pad of paper, when you set out for the course if you hope to approach your favorite players for an autograph. Lots of fans do this, and like everything else in golf, there's a right way and there's a wrong way. Approaching a golfer before he or she starts a round is a bad move. You run the risk of aggravating the golfer or breaking their concentration. And because he or she is probably in a hurry to be on time for tee off, you might get a scribbled autograph, or a grimace from your golf icon, neither of which will make for good memories.

Traditionally, once they're done with their round, golfers head back to the practice area to relax and socialize with other players and fans. Here is the perfect opportunity to request a little meet-and-greet time with the players. Don't be afraid to compliment him or her on a job well done. Let the player know you enjoyed the round or even picked up a tip or two from watching their swing!

First and foremost, remember to be courteous to the players and your fellow spectators. It's not advisable to bring a lot of items to be signed or to monopolize a player's time, especially during the period he or she has set aside for relaxing and cooling down.

Tiger Isn't The Only Animal On This Course

If you're going to be attending an event at Castle Pines Golf Club in Castle Rock, Colorado, you had best keep your eyes open! The course, which was designed by Jack Nicklaus, features a wildlife reserve on the premises that is home to the likes of elk, bobcat, red-tailed hawk and prairie dog.

Well Worth The Price Of Admission

We've given you the basics of watching golf from the gallery, but there's a whole other society involved in the sport of spectating where golf is concerned.

At the PGA Championship, the Corporate Hospitality Chalets are magical places where 50 to 100 guests of corporations can enjoy the tournament and be wined and dined in the process. Located adjacent to the 18th fairway, and available for approximately $155,000, corporations can rent out the Fairway Village Chalet to entertain their clientele and enjoy a week's worth of golf, convenient parking, and other gracious amenities. For another $20,000, a party of 10 can dine at the Corporate Hospitality Table throughout the day for the entire long weekend.

AP/WWP

A young Tiger Woods' fan watches the action at President's Cup.

The U.S. Open features a variety of hospitality tents designed for the comfort of corporate visitors and large parties, also in the range of $130,000 for the week. The air-conditioned tents come equipped with broadcast features, official tournament magazines, merchandise and even get you highly sought-after preferential parking.

Whether you're going for one day or planning to roam the green for the entire event, attending a golf tournament is an exciting experience and is often a once-in-a-lifetime chance. So to maximize your experience, be sure you know all the rules and regulations in advance and plan ahead carefully.

Keeping Up With Tiger

If you're lucky enough to score tickets to a major PGA golf tournament, it's more than likely you're there to see Tiger. Sure, there are other legends of the links, but you've become part of the golf world known as "Tigermania." With hordes of security and strict rules keeping you at a distance, how in the world do you manage to keep up with Tiger?

Tiger Woods' meteoric rise in the golf world is unprecedented in the history of the game. As he piles up win after win, his fans have flocked to tournaments in record numbers. The galleries have become filled with people the likes of which have never been seen in golf – young and old, different races and genders, all cheering for the man they consider one of them.

Tiger watches his drive at the 1997 Ryder Cup.

His Natural Habitat

For most Tiger fans, their dream-come-true is watching him in action live at a tournament. But getting tickets for a PGA event, especially the majors, can be very challenging. Making it even harder is the fact that Tiger sometimes doesn't announce his participation in the smaller events until only weeks before the tournament. And once he makes the announcement, tickets will sell out immediately, so be sure to follow golf news closely.

AP/WWP

Luckily, every year Tiger plays in about 20 PGA events, most of which are in the U.S. (for a listing of the official 2001 PGA tour schedule, see page 170 at the end of this section). Tiger also plays unofficial, international and charity matches every year, so be sure to check for events in your area if your looking to hunt down the ever-elusive Tiger.

Tiger Sightings

Once you've scored those elusive tournament tickets you need to find Tiger. Just follow the crowd! It's difficult to get close to the famous golfer – security is tight. Ropes are set up to keep the crowd a comfortable distance from the players and Tiger has his own security detail in addition to the course's normal security force.

Fans flock to Tiger starting with his arrival in the parking lot all the way until he's come full circle at the end of the day. Most fans like to show up for Tiger's early practice rounds. And once the match starts, Tiger's loyal fans will trail after him from hole to hole hoping for an autograph or a simple "hello" – or if they're really lucky, one of Tiger's patented high-fives. Following Tiger for the entire round can get tiring, so you may want to pick

Simon Bruty/SI/Newsport

Fans watch anxiously as Tiger hits his way out of a sand trap.

out a few strategic holes where you think the best action will take place. You can also get a closer look at Tiger along the paths between the holes.

Catching The "Eye Of The Tiger"

There are many stories of Tiger's warmth toward his younger fans and his preference for kids when it comes to signing autographs. As a matter of fact, it is rare for Tiger to sign any thing for an adult. But that doesn't mean adults can't still hope for a friendly greeting or a flash of his famous smile. Your best bet for a positive response is to wait until after he's made a good shot; as you probably would want to leave him alone if he just got a bogey!

Security looks on as Tiger signs an autograph for a young fan.

AP/WWP

If you wondered why Tiger has so much security with him, it's due to the fact that he's had several incidents with overly aggressive fans. At the PLAYERS CHAMPIONSHIP in 1997, an autograph-seeker accidentally poked him in the eye with a pen and at Bay Hill that same year, one man accidentally hit Tiger in the face with a basketball that he wanted signed.

So remember to be patient, you don't want to go home with Tiger's angry glare as a memory. Also keep in mind that Tiger needs to maintain his focus on the game, and when his round is done, he will be very tired. And he will still have to deal with the media and more fans who wait at his hotel.

Tournament Tickets

To get information about purchasing tickets for PGA events, visit *www.pga.com* or the official website of the particular tournament that you wish to attend.

Tiger On TV

Not everyone can get to see Tiger in person and most must be content watching the matches on television. Seeing him hit one of his great drives or sink a tough putt is fun, but it doesn't get you close to Tiger "the man."

For this, make sure you catch one of his rare television appearances. Tiger likes to keep a low profile, but he's been interviewed by both Oprah Winfrey and Sarah Ferguson (for the *Larry King Live* show) in the past. These are rare times when fans can hear Tiger in his own words. He can also be seen at ESPN's annual ESPY Awards show, accepting everything from Male Athlete of the Year to Golfer of the Year awards.

Tell Tiger How You Feel

You can send fan mail to Tiger through his management group. Write to:

International Management Group
Attn: Tiger Woods
IMG Center, Suite 100
1360 East Ninth Street Cleveland,
Ohio, 44114-1782.

Tiger On The Web

Another great place to "catch" Tiger is on the Internet. His official site (*www.tigerwoods.com*) is full of news updates, yearly tour results and other

Tiger unveils his new website to members of the press.

AP/WWP

goodies for the dedicated fan. And if you still can't get enough, you can join his official fan club (*www.clubtiger.com*) where you can chat with other fans, send Tiger an e-mail and read a column that he writes specifically for his fans.

Tiger Helps Out

From charity golf games to his own Tiger Woods Foundation, Tiger is well-known for giving back to the community. Not only does the Tiger Woods Foundation give money to youth programs all over the country but it also provides young golfers with the chance to meet their idol. Each year as part of the Foundation's Junior Golf Clinics, Tiger visits several cities across the U.S. and gives a lesson to children from local golf groups. A celebrity auction is also held with all the money benefitting programs for under-privileged and minority youth.

Tiger conducts a golf clinic for young golfers in Thailand.

While much of the Tiger Woods Foundation's work is geared towards helping children, the foundation also provides another opportunity for fans to run into Tiger. Every year the Tiger Jam brings in top-name performers and celebrities for a benefit concert, for which tickets are available to the general public. The 2001 Tiger Jam IV raised over $1 million for children's charities, and included guests ranging from Charles Barkley to Kid Rock and Pamela Anderson.

2001 PGA Tour Schedule

Here is a schedule of the 2001 PGA Tour. While Tiger doesn't participate in all of them, you may be able to catch him at some of these events.

January

1-7	World Golf Championships: Accenture Match Play Championship (Melbourne, Australia)
8-14	Mercedes Championships (Kapalua, HI)
8-14	Touchstone Energy Tucson Open (Tucson, AZ)
15-21	Sony Open in Hawaii (Honolulu, HI)
22-28	Phoenix Open (Scottsdale, AZ)
29-2/4	AT&T Pebble Beach National Pro-Am (Pebble Beach, CA)

February

5-11	Buick Invitational (La Jolla, CA)
12-18	Bob Hope Chrysler Classic (La Quinta, CA)
19-25	Nissan Open (Pacific Palisades, CA)
26-28	Genuity Championship (Miami, FL)

March

5-11	The Honda Classic (Coral Springs, FL)
12-18	Bay Hill Invitational (Orlando, FL)
19-25	THE PLAYERS Championship (Ponte Vedra Beach, FL)
26-4/1	BellSouth Classic (Duluth, GA)

April

2-8	Masters Tournament (Augusta, GA)
9-15	WORLDCOM CLASSIC - The Heritage of Golf (Hilton Head Island, SC)
16-22	Shell Houston Open (The Woodlands, TX)
23-29	Greater Greensboro Chrysler Classic (Greensboro, NC)
30-5/6	COMPAQ Classic of New Orleans (New Orleans, LA)

May

7-13	Verizon Byron Nelson Classic (Irving, TX)
14-20	MasterCard Colonial (Fort Worth, TX)
21-27	Kemper Insurance Open (Potomac, MD)
28-6/3	Memorial Tournament (Dublin, OH)

June

4-10	FedEx St. Jude Classic (Memphis, TN)

June, cont.

11-17   U.S. Open (Tulsa, OK)
18-24   Buick Classic (Harrison, NY)
25-7/1   Canon Greater Hartford Open (Cromwell, CT)

July

2-8   Advil Western Open (Lemont, IL)
9-15   Greater Milwaukee Open (Milwaukee, WI)
16-22   British Open (Lytham St. Annes, England)
16-22   B.C. Open (Endicott, NY)
23-29   John Deere Classic (Silvis, IL)
30-8/5   The International (Castle Rock, CO)

August

6-12   Buick Open (Grand Blanc, MI)
13-19   PGA Championship (Duluth, GA)
20-26   World Golf Championships: NEC Invitational (Akron, OH)
20-26   Reno-Tahoe Open (Reno, NV)
27-9/2   Air Canada Championship (Surrey, BC, Canada)

September

3-9   Bell Canadian Open (Montreal, Quebec, Canada)
10-16   Tampa Bay Classic (Palm Harbor, FL)
10-16   World Golf Championships: American Express
         Championship (St. Louis, MO)
17-23   Marconi Pennsylvania Classic (Ligonier, PA)
24-30   Ryder Cup (Sutton, England)
24-30   Texas Open at LaCantera (San Antonio, TX)

October

1-7   Michelob Championship at Kingsmill (Williamsburg, VA)
8-14   Invensys Classic at Las Vegas (Las Vegas, NV)
15-21   National Car Rental Golf Classic at Walt Disney World
         Resort (Lake Buena Vista, FL)
22-28   Buick Challenge (Pine Mountain, GA)
29-11/4 THE TOUR Championship (Houston, TX)
29-11/4 Southern Farm Bureau Classic (Madison, MS)

November

12-18   World Golf Championships: EMC World Cup (Gotemba, Japan)

END OF SEASON

The Endorsement King

They call him "The King," but it's not who you might think. Tiger Woods has mastered the game of golf, but also has surpassed everyone else in sports at another challenging game: product endorsements. He has earned more money than any other professional athlete, including Michael Jordan. When it comes to commercials, Tiger Woods reigns supreme as "The Endorsement King."

Tiger Woods has established himself as perhaps the premier player in all of golf, and some would say, all of sports. He has even captured titles in all four major tournaments. But there's another record being set by Tiger. In 2000, Tiger surpassed sports mega-star Michael Jordan in endorsement earnings, by garnering a reported $54 million for his various sponsorships. This makes him the highest paid athlete ever for commercial work. What makes him so valuable that companies are willing to spend millions of dollars for a mere 30 seconds of air time featuring golf's newest legend? Who would have thought any golfer could command such power in the advertising world?

AP/WWP

Tiger beams at the annoucement making him the international spokesperson for American Express.

Blue Suede Golf Shoes

"He's Elvis. We've found Elvis and he looks like Tiger Woods," said Rick Burton, director of the Warsaw Sports Marketing Center at the University of Oregon. When he turned pro in 1996, Tiger penned million-dollar deals with Nike and Titleist. The ads Nike ran introduced the general public to Tiger and he quickly became a household name. In the commercials, young boys and girls of every race and culture chanted, "I am Tiger Woods." As Tiger began to dominate the pro tour, the public grew fascinated with this young sport prodigy. The commercials let people "come into his world a little bit," said Mark Steinberg, Tiger's agent.

After five years as a pro and many championships under his belt – including what some would call golf's "Grand Slam" – Tiger signed a new contract with Nike for $100 million in 2000. He also has lucrative contracts with General Motors, American Express, video game manufacturer EA Sports, Rolex, General Mills and Japan's Asahi Beer. Is it surprising that a golfer would make so much money and have such a powerful effect on the American public? "It doesn't surprise me at all," said Earl Woods, Tiger's father. "He's worth every bit of it. And when the next contract comes around, this one will look like chump change and peanuts compared to that one."

The business of handling Tiger Woods is so extensive that his management company, International Management Group, has what it terms "Team Tiger" to coordinate his deals with his endorsement companies. But, you may wonder, what makes him so valuable?

Tiger Spreads It Around

Tiger has been known to donate portions of his winnings to charity. After winning the Masters in 2001, he reportedly gave all the prize money to the Tiger Woods Foundation.

In The Game

As with any sport, there's always the danger of injury cutting a golfer's career short. However, Tiger's father Earl sees no end in sight for the success of his superstar son. "The sky's the limit," says Earl, "as long as he's injury free."

Charisma And Longevity

Virtually everyone knows Tiger, whether they're golf fans or not. As he relates to many different cultures and demographics, he has become an international sensation, and has drawn fans to the game that never would have been interested before his rise.

In advertising, marketers often look at demographics to attract certain groups of people to their commercials and, ultimately, their products. Tiger transcends any limited demographic, mainly because of his own mixed-race background, but also because of his charismatic, broad-based appeal. He attracts young and old alike, women and men and people all across the economic scale. There is no limit to his appeal and for corporations wanting to sell products from sneakers to cars, he is priceless.

The Billion Dollar Man

In July 2000, *ESPN The Magazine* reported that Tiger's lifetime earnings are expected to reach $6 billion in tournament winnings and endorsements. Seventy-five percent of this money, they said, will be from the endorsements.

Tiger might play golf for the rest of his life, which gives his name and image incredible longevity. Unlike other professional athletes, who typically retire before age 40, golfers can continue to play at a high level well into their later years. If he can avoid injuries, Tiger should be wowing galleries for the next 30 or 40 more years. Many golfers like Jack Nicklaus or Arnold Palmer, who peaked in the 1960s, still enjoy big endorsement contracts, as well as name recognition and continued popularity. Tiger began his career at an early age and will be active for as long as he wants to be. This translates into many more years of lucrative advertising revenues for his endorsements. "You can expect Tiger Woods to become a fixture in American life for the next thirty years," predicts Brian Murphy, publisher of the *Sports Marketing Letter*.

Why's Tiger so happy? Because he's the new Buick spokesperson!

Ratings King

Another reason behind Tiger's enormous value is his impact on television ratings. He doubles and triples ratings for the tournaments he plays, according to official network estimates. When Tiger tried for his seventh straight win at the Buick Open in February 2000, the ratings for that tournament topped the NBA All-Star Game, which was broadcast simultaneously. NBC's ratings for Tiger's win at the U.S. Open in 2000 rose 19% over the year before, when Payne Stewart made his incredible finish on the final hole. Estimates from NBC had 53 million people watching on that weekend, the highest rating for any U.S. Open in almost 20 years.

Neilsen's Golden Boy

"Tiger single-handedly can move a rating on a Sunday 40 to 50 percent," said Rob Correa, vice president of programming for CBS Sports. "No other athlete in any other sport can have the impact he does, let alone another golfer."

The increased ratings attract more sponsors to golf events, which in turn offer more potential for endorsements for the athletes. But Tiger has also attracted non-golf corporations to the tournaments in which he plays. This helps other golfers, too, as the increased revenue being pumped into golf endorsements means more contracts for other players. Players are seen sporting the logos of companies they represent on their hats and clothes. Many players use clubs and balls made by the top equipment manufacturers to show their endorsement of those products. Tiger's own image is almost inseparable from the Nike swoosh which graces his baseball caps.

Follow The Bouncing Ball

Tiger is known for his now famous Nike ad, where he bounces a golf ball on his club for several seconds, after which he sends it sailing away with a baseball swing of his club. What many people don't know is that this ad came to be strictly by accident!

Unwound

A Nike representative recently commented on the impact Tiger's preferences have had on the quality of the Nike golf ball. He said, "You know, we were just a small player in the golf ball category. And when Tiger switched, it just raised the level and the bar, so to speak, in terms of our expectations for the golf ball. And when he switched from a wound ball to a non-wound ball, it sent shockwaves through the industry."

Tiger was on the set filming an ad for Nike in which he joins a driving range full of people taking terrible swings at balls. After he steps up to the tee, people start watching him and slowly everyone at the range falls into sync with him, their hacks becoming beautiful swings that propel their balls 300 yards. The commercial was directed by Lasse Hallstrom, who directed the Academy Award-winning film *The Cider House Rules* and Academy Award nominee *Chocolat*. He spotted Tiger during a break entertaining the crew by bouncing a golf ball on his club. In a moment of inspiration, the director filmed Tiger performing this trick. Just four takes and eight minutes later, advertising history was made. Nike loved the spot and the ad became an instant classic.

But there was one company who didn't think much of the ad. Tiger was under contract with Titleist, the leading manufacturer of golf balls, at the time. Titleist sued Nike, saying the ad implied that Tiger used Nike golf balls. At the time, Tiger was using Titleist because of his endorsement contract with them. However, Nike had introduced its own ball, which was lagging in sales. Eventually, Titleist dropped the suit and Tiger began using Nike balls for his tournament play. And no one was shocked when Nike ball sales increased dramatically soon after.

Will Tiger soon be putting the other famous cereal tiger icon out of a job?

Multimedia Giant

Some of Tiger's other big endorsement deals are with American Express, EA Sports and Disney. Tiger runs clinics sponsored by American Express and for EA Sports, he helped design a game with his name on it. In 2001, Tiger inked a big deal with the Walt Disney Company. He will endorse merchandise for Disney, work for Disney-owned ESPN and appear in ads promoting the entertainment giant's theme parks.

One of the ways Tiger maintains his endorsement value is by being choosy about who he sponsors. He has limited his deals to a handful of companies and is very hands-on in the negotiations of what he will and won't do for them. This way he can demand the highest price for his endorsements, while at the same time not over-commercializing his image with the public.

"It's Good To Be The King!"

But with all these companies bidding on him, will the money eventually ruin Tiger? Some say he's still too young to be so wealthy. However, his father says success will not spoil Tiger. "For Tiger, it's never been about the money," says Earl Woods. "His performance isn't going to drop off just because he signs a deal or earns a certain amount of money. Tiger has no comfort zone when it comes to competition."

Apparently, there is no comfort zone for anyone else when it comes to competing with Tiger, on the course or with the public. We can't get enough of this guy and from the looks of it, he'll be around for a long while, wowing us on the links and constantly amazing us with his style and grace off the links. Long live "The Endorsement King!"

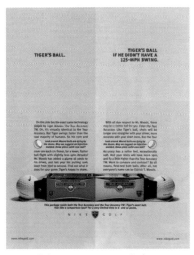

One of the many print ads featuring Tiger Woods' line of Nike products.

Tiger's Products

If you're looking for the best in Tiger Woods gear and products, look no further than the following pages to find everything you need to show that you're a fan of golf's young great.

With his golfing prowess and youthful charm, 25-year-old Tiger Woods is the darling of not only golf fans, but marketing executives everywhere. Companies like Nike have snatched Tiger up to endorse their products, developing lines like Nike's TW Collection of apparel and golf gear. Other companies have gotten in on the act as well, and it's now possible to find items like video games and posters bearing Tiger's image or stamp of approval. So check out this great Tiger gear and keep your eyes peeled – there are many other Tiger-related products out there just waiting for you.

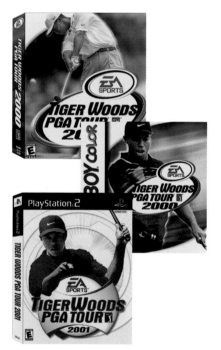

Computer Games

As a lifelong fan of computer games – he reportedly spends his down time relaxing with rousing games of *Mortal Kombat* – Tiger has made sure that his fans can hit the links right alongside him, digitally!

Tiger's fans can play as Tiger or match their skills against the "master" in *Tiger Woods PGA Tour 2001* and the older 2000 edition, both for PlayStation and PC and available from EA Sports™. For the gamer on the go, there's even a Gameboy version.

Apparel

When Tiger first went pro and his star began to rise, Nike knew it would be smart to get in on Tiger-mania and issue some Tiger-related clothes. But no matter how successful fan T-shirts and designer sneakers may have been for basketball, the traditional world of golf just wasn't ready to endorse such highly casual attire. No one would have even *thought* about wearing a T-shirt and sneakers to the U.S. Open!

But Tiger's own classy-yet-relaxed style has prompted Nike to release a brand new line of sportswear with the game of golf in mind. This time, Tiger has a line of clothing you'd be proud to wear at the Masters Tournament – provided they go with the Green Jacket, of course!

The Nike TW Collection's stylish shirts come in muted colors such as gray and navy (as well as Tiger's signature final round red) while the distinctive vests and warm sweaters add a touch of class. If it gets too sunny at the tournament, you can always block out the rays with an ultra-cool pair of Tiger Woods sunglasses and shade your face with one of his signature baseball caps, each one bearing Nike's logo.

With such a great collection, Tiger's fans can look their best, whether they're hitting the links on Saturday or at the office on "Casual Friday!"

Golf Equipment

Even a golfer as great as Tiger needs the right equipment. And with Nike's TW collection on the market, fans can take some of Tiger's favorite equipment out on the course with them.

Walking the course all day can tire you out in a hurry, so it's important to wear comfortable shoes. Tiger's TW Course Air line, which features waterproof leather and Gore-Tex, is ideal for hitting the links.

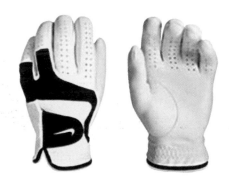

When you're trying to drive the ball for a hole-in-one on the 18th hole, having your club slip out of your hands could be quite a nuisance. That's why dedicated golfers wear gloves. To help Tiger's fans "get a grip" on their game, Nike has released a series of Tiger-endorsed golf gloves. True Tiger devotees can choose from two different styles, designed to keep those clubs where they belong – in your hands!

After you have all your equipment together, don't forget the ball. Nike also makes golf balls, designed to Tiger's exact specifications. Think you can outdrive Tiger? Don't bet on it!

Posters

When you combine a telegenic media sensation like Tiger with the beauty of the world's best golf courses, you've got the perfect ingredients for a great poster!

With companies like Titleist and Nike (among others) producing posters of different sizes and styles, there's something to please everyone. Artistic renderings of Tiger, black-and-white photos, or action shots will please every Tiger fan in the gallery. There's even one with his advice on golf – but, if you and Tiger ever play against each other, don't expect those hints to make it any easier to beat him!

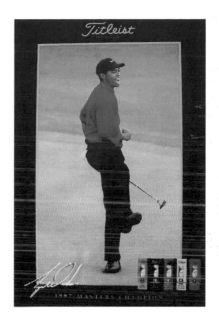

Videos

Wouldn't you have loved to have been at the 2000 British Open and seen Tiger complete his career Grand Slam? Unfortunately, airfare to Scotland doesn't come cheap.

But there's still a way to experience some of Tiger's most shining career moments. With such important tournaments as the 1997 Masters and the 2000 U.S. Open available on VHS, you can relive Tiger's victories again and again.

If you're interested in Tiger's life story, check out the documentary, *Tiger Woods – The Heart Of A Champion* or the movie, *The Tiger Woods Story*.

Other Golf Products

For many people, golf is a sacred sport. They live to play it, and can't wait to get on the links or tune in to the latest PGA tournament.

But the love of golf goes far beyond the game itself, and even Tiger! A whole world of products for the golf collector as well as the golf pro have hit the market in recent years.

When buying a tournament ticket, you can use your USGA money clip to hold your change together. And no matter what the weather's like on tournament day, a commemorative U.S. Open umbrella can help you weather Augusta's harshest sunlight or a nasty rainfall. After the tournament's over, you can withdraw to the clubhouse and drink a refreshing brew from a golf pilsner glass or beer mug as you regale your golfing buddies with the story of how you sank a 50-foot putt to birdie on the 18th hole last week. Well, a little embellishment never hurt.

Creative designers have also come up with just about everything to make the golf fan's office more bearable. From business card holders to golf-themed ties, you can take your hobby to work, right under the boss' nose.

And, if all else fails, there's always the golf Monopoly game to amuse you when it's too rainy to hit the links.

Tiger Memorabilia

As Tiger continues to rewrite the record books, some of his memorabilia is becoming coveted by collectors assuming that as his legend grows, so will the values of their collections.

Whatever your interest, there's sure to be some Tiger memorabilia for you. Programs and tickets from some of the events Tiger has won have been hot on the collectibles market, as have magazines featuring Tiger on their covers. And keep an eye out for Tiger on your grocery store shelves, as the Wheaties boxes he's appeared on are now coveted by collectors.

Be a cautious shopper, however. Given Tiger's incredible popularity, it's not hard to find unauthorized or counterfeit material. As with any collectible, make sure you're getting what you're paying for!

Trading Cards

In addition to the great Upper Deck cards available in June 2001, collectors can try their luck at these rarities.

1996 *Sports Illustrated For Kids* Trading Card

	Values
1996 *Sports Illustrated For Kids* (insert)	N/E
1997 Grand Slam Ventures (rookie card)	N/E
1999 *Sports Illustrated For Kids* (insert)	N/E
2001 *Sports Illustrated For Kids* (insert, set/4)	$175

Magazine Covers

He might be the most photographed athlete in the world! This is a very small sampling of Tiger-covered magazines.

April 3, 2000 *Sports Illustrated* with "Tiger Rules" cover

	Values
Dec. 23, 1996 *Sports Illustrated* ("Sportsman of the Year")	$75
Oct. 28, 1996 *Sports Illustrated*	$35
Apr. 3, 2000 *Sports Illustrated* ("Tiger Rules")	N/E
Apr. 16, 2001 *Sports Illustrated* (The Masters)	$25
1995 *Stanford Magazine*	$45
1997 *Year of the Tiger* (Commemorative Magazine)	$25

Cereal Boxes

Another great reason to eat your Wheaties – Tiger's Wheaties boxes are highly collectible!

1998 "Our Newest Champion" Crispy Wheaties 'n Raisins box

	Values
1998 Crispy Wheaties 'n Raisins ("Our Newest Champion")	$20
1998 Honey Frosted Wheaties (with trophy)	$18
1998 Wheaties (3 golf balls free)	$18
2000 Wheaties Mini 24K Gold Signature	$36

Tickets & Programs

If you're lucky enough to get to a PGA event with Tiger on the docket, save your programs and tickets!

Tickets to the 2000 U.S. Open at Pebble Beach

	Values
1997 Masters Ticket	.$500*
2000 PGA Tournament Ticket	.$135*
2000 U.S. Open Ticket	.$110*
2000 U.S. Open Program	. . . .$25
2000 British Open Program	. . . .$28

* values are for intact, unused tickets

2000 U.S. Open Program

Other Memorabilia

From the "potpourri" department comes these collectibles that would make any Tiger Woods fan smile.

	Values
1997 Turkmenistan Stamps (3)	.$400
2001 Madagascar Stamps (sheet of 9)	.$50
Celebrity Bear Star #12 Bean Bag Bear	.$18
Tiger On The 18th Hole Figurine (benefits Tiger Woods Foundation)	.N/E
Tiger Woods Rolex Watch . .	.$3,500

Madagascar Stamps (sheet of nine)

Tiger Woods Chronograph Rolex Watch

Autographed Items

Items that have been personally autographed by Tiger can fetch a pretty penny. Here are some examples of hand-signed Tiger items and their values.

Hand-signed 2001 Masters Flag

2000 U.S. Open Flag	$650
2001 Masters Flag	N/E
1998 PGA Tour Program	$350
2000 U.S. Open Program	$300
Nike Ball	N/E
Titleist Ball	N/E
8 x 10 Photo	$100
Nike Hat	N/E

General Golf Memorabilia

The Tiger Woods memorabilia available really just scratches the surface of the world of golf memorabilia. There are all kinds of collectibles and memorabilia devoted to other golfers and the sport in general.

Framed lithographs and prints commemorating a special moment in the golfer's career are popular. Vintage golf clubs, bags and other equipment appeal to those taken with the game's rich heritage, while mint, first-edition golf books attract golfers and book collectors alike.

Unique items, such as clubs and other equipment used by the golfers (sometimes signed) are the rarest of the rare! It's not unusual for these treasures to be put up for auction, sometimes for charity.

Framed photo commemorating a Tiger's U.S. Open victory.

A Golf Glossary

Think birdies and eagles are simply feathered creatures that fly around in the sky? Then maybe you'd better brush up on your golf terminology before heading out to the links.

19th hole – commonly used slang for the clubhouse bar.

ace – another term for a hole-in-one.

address – the stance a player takes right before hitting the ball.

approach – a shot made to the green but not from the tee.

apron – the slightly longer grass surrounding the green; also known as the "collar" or the "fringe."

back nine – the last nine holes of the course.

birdie – when a player scores 1 under par for a hole.

bogey – when a player scores 1 over par for a hole.

bunker – a course hazard filled with sand; also known as a "sand trap."

caddie – individuals who carry the player's clubs and provide advice during play.

chip – a short, low shot made to the green.

chip-in – a chip shot which goes in the hole.

cup – the container inside the hole.

divot – a clump of sod or turf that is torn up when a player hits the ball. Golf etiquette requires you to replace the divot.

dogleg – a hole on the course which has a curved fairway.

double bogey – a score of 2 over par for a hole.

double eagle – a score of 3 under par for a hole.

drive – a shot hit for maximum distance, usually from the tee with a driver.

duffer – a bad player, also known as a "hacker."

casual water – water on the course that is not a hazard. There is no penalty for hitting into it.

cut – a score that eliminates players from the tournament, typically after 36 holes.

eagle – a score of 2 strokes under par for a hole.

extra holes – holes played to break a tie.

fairway – the area between the tee and the green.

front nine – the first nine holes of the course.

gallery – the crowd of spectators at a tournament.

Grand Slam – winning all four of the major tournaments (Masters Tournament, U.S. Open, British Open and the PGA Championship) in the same year.

green – the area of short-cut grass surrounding the hole.

Green Jacket – the special jacket that is given to the winner of the Masters Tournament.

greens fee – the money you pay a golf course to play.

handicap – an allowance of strokes given to a player based on their past performance that is designed to level the playing field.

hazard – an obstruction on the course, usually filled with sand (see **bunker**) or water, to make the course more challenging.

hole-in-one – a shot which goes straight from the tee into the hole.

iron – flat, iron or steel-headed clubs which are typically numbered. The larger the number, the higher in the air the ball will go. The smaller the number, the farther the ball will go. This category also includes wedges and putters.

lay-up – a shot that is played conservatively.

lie – the position of your ball on the ground.

links – originally used to describe traditional seaside courses, the term is now commonly used to refer to any type of course.

lip – the edge of the cup or hole.

lob – a shot that goes straight up and back down again.

lost ball – if you lose sight of your ball and cannot find it after five minutes of searching, it is considered a "lost ball" and you are given a penalty.

marshal – an individual who is in charge of controlling the crowd during an event.

match play – often played in teams of two or two players pitted against each other, the winner of this type of event has won the most holes. (see **stroke play**).

misread – to misinterpret the angle of a putt and hit it in the wrong direction.

open tournament – these events allow amateurs golfers to compete alongside professionals.

out of bounds – if a ball goes outside the boundary markers, it is considered out of bounds and the player receives a penalty.

par – the standard number of strokes assigned to a hole. This is the score that a golfer should hope to achieve (or better) for each hole.

penalty strokes – additional strokes added to a player's score as a penalty for things like going out of bounds or hitting into a hazard.

pitch – a short, high shot not meant to roll very far when it lands, like that used to exit a sand trap.

Pro-Am – this kind of tournament pairs professionals with amateurs.

provisional ball – a replacement ball if your original ball is lost.

putt – to hit the ball when it's on the green.

putt out – to get the ball in the hole on a putt.

rough – area on either side of the fairway where the grass is longer.

round – a full 18 holes of golf.

run – the roll of a ball after it lands.

scratch player – a player with a zero handicap.

slice – a shot that curves from left to right.

straightaway – a hole with a straight fairway.

stroke – moving the club with the intent of hitting the ball.

stroke play – also known as "medal play," this is the standard method of play used in tournaments. The winner completes the event with the least number of strokes (see **match play**).

sudden-death – a playoff match where the first player to win a hole wins the event.

tee – the wooden or plastic peg where the ball rests at the beginning of the hole. Also refers to the area where the tee shot is made.

triple bogey – a score of 3 over par for a hole.

waggle – the movement of the golf club just before the swing.

wedge – a club used to hit the ball a short distance, but high in the air. For example, a sand wedge, which is used to hit the ball out of a bunker.

wood – a type of numbered club, including the driver, with a large head used for hitting long distances. Though traditionally wood, most of these clubs are now metal, despite the name.

Photo Index

Use this index to find photographs of the individuals depicted in this book.

Braid, James 120

Chang, Jerry 65

Couples, Fred. 123

Daly, John 141

Davis, Bob 23

DiMarco, Chris 18

Duval, David 20, 149

Edmonds, Kenneth "Babyface" . 66

Elder, Lee. 59

Els, Ernie 150

Faldo, Nick 40, 105, 124, 141

Fleck, Jack. 37

Floyd, Ray 124

Garcia, Sergio 51, 151

Hagen, Walter 43, 124

Harmon, Butch 68, 89

Havemeyer, Theodore 35

Herd, Sandy. 120

Hogan, Ben. 33, 114, 125

Irwin, Hale. 139

January, Don 44

Jones, Bobby 31, 121, 125

Jones, Robert T., IV 23

Kim, Mi Hyun 137

Laird, Anne Hood 23

Lopez, Nancy 125

Love, Davis III. 151

Maise, Mickey 69

Matthew, Sidney 23

May, Bob 45

Mickelson, Phil 17, 152

Morland, David 133

Morris, Tom, Sr. 39

Nelson, Byron 126

Nicklaus, Jack 9, 53, 126

Norman, Greg 126